Ideology and Art

American University Studies

Series V
Philosophy

Vol. 6

PETER LANG
New York · Berne · Frankfort on the Main · Nancy

Robin Ridless

Ideology and Art

Theories of Mass Culture from Walter Benjamin to Umberto Eco

PETER LANG
New York · Berne · Frankfort on the Main · Nancy

Library of Congress Cataloging in Publication Data

Ridless, Robin, 1950–
  Ideology and art.
  (American University Studies. Series V, Philosophy; v. 6)
  Bibliographie: p.
  1. Popular culture – Evaluation. 2. Aesthetics – Political aspects. 3. Frankfurt school of sociology. 4. Structuralism. 5. Mass media and the arts. 6. Ideology. I. Title. II. Series.
HM101.R49 1984   306'.47   84-47698
ISBN 0-8204-0124-2

CIP-Kurztitelaufnahme der Deutschen Bibliothek

Ridless, Robin:
Ideology and art: theories of mass culture from Walter Benjamin to Umberto Eco / Robin Ridless. – New York; Berne; Frankfort on the Main; Nancy: Lang, 1984.
  (American University Studies: Ser. 5, Philosophy; Vol. 6)
  ISBN 0-8204-0124-2

NE: American University Studies / 05

© Peter Lang Publishing, Inc., New York 1984

All rights reserved.
Reprint or reproduction, even partially, in all forms such as microfilm, xerography, microfiche, microcard, offset prohibited.

Printed by Lang Druck Inc., Liebefeld/Berne (Switzerland)

TABLE OF CONTENTS

PREFACE		vi
INTRODUCTION		vii
Chapter I.	WALTER BENJAMIN: THE CHANGING OF THE SUPERSTRUCTURE	1
Chapter II.	BERTOLT BRECHT: THE AUTHOR AS PRODUCER	61
Chapter III.	AUTONOMOUS CULTURE: SURVIVING MESSAGE OF THE SHIPWRECKED	93
Chapter IV.	UMBERTO ECO AND "SOCIAL LIFE AS A SIGN-SYSTEM"	145
Chapter V.	ROLAND BARTHES: THE UNCULTURE OF IDEOLOGY	177
CONCLUSION	MECHANICAL REPRODUCTION IN THE AGE OF MECHANICAL REPRODUCTION	203
SELECTED BIBLIOGRAPHY		229

PREFACE

I would like to acknowledge the following people:

Mark Elber, who gave me the strength to be myself;

Betty Hellman, who taught me how;

Vara Neverow-Turk, who taught me how to write, even though she says there is no such thing;

And my parents, who supported me.

INTRODUCTION

The 1930's saw a great deal of debate among leading German Marxist theorists in the area of aesthetics. Georg Lukacs, Ernst Bloch, Theodor Adorno, Walter Benjamin and Bertolt Brecht were all active contributors.[1] Their writings take off in every direction from the nucleus of a general assumption: that art is, in some manner or form, political. Stemming from a common Hegelian heritage, in which "universal mind" reaches its potential in the context of the state through the instrumentalities of art, religion and philosophy, the belief prevailed among them that art was both a product and a reflection of the social totality of which it was a part.[2] The question they pursued, then, was never "Is art political?" or "Does art reflect the basic social and economic facts of capitalist society?"--a question to which they would have unanimously assented--but rather "Which art is progressive, which reactionary?" Or to clarify those ambiguous terms, "Which art expresses and promotes a revolutionary working class consciousness and which obscures the fundamental nature of class and

---

[1] Ernst Bloch et al., Aesthetics and Politics, trans. and ed. Ronald Taylor (London: New Left Books, 1977).

[2] G. W. F. Hegel, Hegel's Philosophy of Right, T. M. Knox (London: Oxford University Press, 1967), pp. 216-24.

property relations in modern industrial society?"

In Europe, the onset of modernism in the arts made the answer to this question far from self-evident. The Marxist controversy was over realism, and it was precipitated by the invention of its opposite, abstractionism. Since the last quarter of the nineteenth century, modern art had been insulting traditional canons of bourgeois beauty by reproducing the world in a mode which, by earlier standards, was bound to seem highly fragmented, clashing, distorted. It was clear that abstraction in the plastic arts and dissonance and atonality in music had the power to shock and outrage middle-class audiences. What was less clear was what these innovations were saying about the world once a person got past their audacious novelty. How were Marxists supposed to decipher them in light of their great concern for revolutionary change--not just in art, but in society at large?

Lukacs maintained a fairly stationary (Soviet inspired) opposition to the new art, providing a fixed point against which the others could define themselves contrapuntally. His heroes were the great epic novelists of the nineteenth century (Balzac, Tolstoy) and what was for him their twentieth-century counterpart, Thomas Mann. His main argument was that art should reproduce life verily, in all of its complex mediations, in its "immanent meaning." Though the artist must abstract from raw historical material in order to depict it, he is also obligated to cover up his tracks, to portray "life as it actually appears." The modern artist, by contrast, repeats the dissociated perception of the alienated individual under capitalism. He divorces the subjective from the objective. Only an organic art reconstructs ". . . the whole surface of life in all its essential determinants, and not just a subjectively perceived moment isolated from the totality in an abstract and over-intense manner."[3]

The others disagreed that there was no value in rendering the world as it appeared to contemporary consciousness. Modern art was an inventive way of giving contradiction outline and thus exposing its presence and resonances in everyday life. It gave expression not only to subjective feeling, but to a developing, changing reality. ". . . What if Lukacs' reality--a coherent, infinitely mediated totality --is not so objective after all? . . . What if authentic reality is also discontinuity?"[4] Ernst Bloch wonders. If this is the case, he maintained, then "disruptive and interpolative" techniques like montage are best designed to capture the shattered world of capitalism. Such art

---

[3]George Lukacs, "Realism in the Balance," in Bloch et al., *Aesthetics and Politics*, p. 39.

[4]Ibid., p. 22.

might be able to find what there is on the other side of alienation.[5]

The perspective of the Frankfurt School elaborated on this sympathy with avant-garde art. Adorno retained as the foundation of his aesthetic a distinction between autonomous and commodity art, which was developed by Herbert Marcuse in a 1937 essay, "The Affirmative Character of Culture."[6] The distinction corresponded not only to two different kinds of art, but to two different methods of analyzing them. The autonomous work of art was one whose formal integrity was vouchsafed by its utter lack of compromise with the market. Its truth resided in its construction and thus required a direct, compositional analysis to rationalize. On the other hand, simulacra of autonomous works, near-misses (Stravinsky), were also to be analyzed, first, to expose the deformation within, and second, to interpolate from it to the existence of social interests and bourgeois competition.

---

[5] Ibid., p. 22.

[6] Herbert Marcuse defined "affirmative culture" as ". . . culture of the bourgeois epoch which led in the course of its own development to the segregation from civilization of the mental and spiritual world as an independent realm of value that is also considered superior to civilization. Its decisive characteristic is the assertion of a universally obligatory, eternally better, and more valuable world that must be unconditionally affirmed: a world essentially different from the factual world of the daily struggle for existence, yet realizable by every individual for himself 'from within', without any transformation of the state of fact. . . ." in <u>Negations: Essays in Critical Theory</u> trans. Jeremy J. Shapiro (Boston: Beacon Press, 1968).

Adorno's ideal of autonomous art was the music of Arnold Schoenberg, inventor of the twelve-tone scale:

> Its truth appears guaranteed more by its denial of any meaning in organized society, of which it will have no part--accomplished by its own organized vacuity--than by any capability of positive meaning within itself. Under the present circumstances, it is restricted to definitive negation.[7]

For an artistic content to remain indigestible to society was both the proof and consequence of its autonomy. No matter how much time passes, we will not be likely to hear a Schoenberg score on one of our "beautiful music" stations.

Dependent art did not warrant formal analysis, only exposure of its psychological aftereffects. A critique of mass culture, or "the culture industry" as Horkheimer and Adorno significantly dubbed it in the Dialectic of Enlightenment, played an important part in the School's analysis of Nazism.[8] Mass culture's power to evoke conformity, to keep the consumer's responses at an arrested, "infantile" state, to manipulate him or her with false promises of libidinal gratification--these same conclusions were invoked again and again in the Institute for Social Research's empirical studies of commercial culture. The objects of study varied, but the evidence always pointed to mass culture's role in

---

[7] T. D. Adorno, The Philosophy of Modern Music (New York: Seabury Press, 1973), p. 20.

[8] Martin Jay, The Dialectical Imagination: A History of the Frankfurt School and the Institute of Social Research, 1923-50 (Boston: Little, Brown & Co., 1973), pp. 160-66.

priming the people for demagogic takeover.[9]

Adorno's double standard may be seen quite clearly by comparing two roughly contemporaneous pieces of music criticism, written by him for the Institute's journal in the early 1930's. One was a pilot essay on Schoenberg that would eventually appear in The Philosophy of Modern Music; the other was entitled, "On Jazz." Lacking in the geometrical complexity of twelve-tone combinations, explicated at great length in the former, jazz's native rhythms were peremptorily dismissed as empty repetition in the latter. Repetition was then associated with emotional passivity. (Later, he will describe such repetition with the term "slave rhythms.") This leaves many questions unanswered, including those pertaining to experimental, non-commodity forms of repetition. The latter arise out of the same material necessity as popular culture, but for that very reason serve as a critique and clarification of that other, neurotic kind that Adorno is talking about.[10]

By reading totalitarianism and persuasion into all mass art (and by inspiring American social scientists like

---

[9] T. D. Adorno, "A Social Critique of Radio Music," Kenyon Review VII, 2 (Spring, 1945); "On Popular Music," Studies in Philosophy and Social Science IX, 1 (1941); "How to Look at Television," The Quarterly of Film, Radio and Television VIII (1954); Max Horkheimer, "Art and Mass Culture," SPSS IX, 2 (1941).

[10] For example, the music of Steve Reich. See also Jay, The Dialectical Imagination, pp. 180-87.

William Kornhauser and David Riesman to do likewise),[11] Adorno evinced a profound indifference to the possibility that a progressive commercial culture might exist (even if we define "progressive" here as that music which leads its listeners out of itself and toward the kind of music Adorno sanctions). It was around this time that rock and roll was swelling into a national movement. Its growth occurred in opposition to the corporate entertainment industry--an opposition that was reflected both in the music and in its instruments of production and distribution.[12] In their multifarious studies of radio, film, and television, the members of the Institute never mentioned the differential treatment being handed to rock and roll by the culture industry. It is unsurprising. As long as commercial mass art continued to be categorized homogeneously, the chance that some art symbolically subverted or commented on other art, within a single market context, would remain indistinct. To maintain that beside high and low art there is a relevant opposition between good and bad low art, appropriate criteria, formal taxonomies, would have to be developed, as they were in Adorno's criticism of high culture. Marxist

---

[11] William Kornhauser, The Politics of Mass Society (New York: The Free Press, 1959), Ch. 2; Leon Bramson, The Political Context of Sociology (Princeton: Princeton University Press, 1961).

[12] This has only begun to be documented in an emerging pop historiography. See Dave Marsh, Born to Run (Garden City, New York: Doubleday, 1979).

aesthetic theory would have to submit to some retooling, if it were to comprehend the individuality of mass-produced art.

It might be argued that this is what Walter Benjamin and Bertolt Brecht were up to. Both men felt that the realism question had been put on a different footing with the advancement of communications technologies. Benjamin argued that the venerable, tradition-laden object of classical bourgeois culture had become stripped of its "aura," its inimitability, through the ease and exactitude of copying made possible by "mechanical reproduction." The function of art adapted accordingly. From ritual, "the location of art's original use value," and the "secular cult of beauty," it shifted to documentation of the world through its perfect reproduction. The realism that resulted from photography and film transformed the beguiled artworshipper of old into the critical viewer of today. Art became correspondingly less ideological and more aligned with the political as a result of the transition.[13]

All the theorists we will be looking at granted that a deep rift existed between past and popular culture. Walter Benjamin was more or less at ease with the fact that mass culture had begun to blaze its own trail. When he analyzed mechanical reproduction and the ruin of the aura, he was documenting

---

[13] Walter Benjamin, "The Work of Art in the Age of Mechanical Reproduction," in Illuminations, ed. Hannah Arendt (New York: Schocken Books, 1969), pp. 217-52.

a whole new way of perceiving and experiencing the world. What he was describing was the cognitive transformation that accompanied the institutional transformation of advanced industrial society. The change he described lay chiefly in the loss of individuality. Such loss was across-the-board. In production, culture is now created through a cooperative, specialized effort comparable to the industrial labor process. In reception, the individual is ignited by the crowd. In perception, the object is known through its double and not its unique essence. That Benjamin was, indeed, speaking about a new episteme, or field of knowledge, is clear in his linking perception in the age of mechanical reproduction to statistics. Our capacity to analyze human relations quantitatively, to design institutions on the basis of numerical calculations of masses of data, depends on the same de-individualization that makes television images absolutely real and present to their viewers. Benjamin accepted this greatly altered culture on its own terms. Whatever its liabilities, the decline of spirituality being foremost among them, they are able to be compensated for with mechanical reproduction. Benjamin did not yearn for conservative solutions. The thrust of his argument was that the anatomy of art has changed, and so has the seat of its value. The escape routes from bourgeois mass culture must be sought within what already exists.

Adorno could not resign himself as gracefully to

the passing of traditional culture, although he mourned its inevitability. He often looks at the same phenemona as Benjamin and calls them by different, more pejorative names. For instance, popular music's reliance on statistical research is "propagandistic," whereas, for Benjamin, it is symptomatic of a shared structure. Or the behavior of the modern audience is "dehumanized," disassociated, schizophrenic; for Benjamin, it is usefully distracted. (Distraction can be seen as a subliminal means of assimilating information, or as a fracture of the strongly centered self. Adorno sees it the second way, as a harbinger of totalitarianism. Benjamin explains it the first way, as part and parcel of a valuable post-individualism.)

Benjamin's thought is like a tapestry. If you throw the light of Adorno's criticism on it, you see one configuration of shapes; that of Brecht, and you see quite another. Adorno responds to Benjamin by letter from New York after reading the manuscript of "The Work of Art in the Age of Mechanical Reproduction." He is disturbed by what he sees as Benjamin's romanticism, imputing it to the influence of his friend, Bertolt Brecht. He tries to persuade him to "liquidate" it and reminds him that after tradition comes not post-capitalist art, but Mickey Mouse. In other words, the realism that Benjamin celebrates is a pseudo-realism. It is thoroughly imbued with commodity values, even at the level of its supposedly objective form.

Under a Brechtian illumination, other possibilities are silhouetted, principally the potential of a strategic, as opposed to a literal, realism. Brecht concluded, <u>contra</u> Lukacs, that the theatrical use of film and other modern media was demanded by the global and entangling relations of capitalism. How else could the "micro" events taking place on stage be socially situated, if not with screen projections telling the "macro" story simultaneously? Yet normal forms of representation had to become studied, unfamiliar, in a word, distorted, in order that their prejudicing of our thought be thrown into "observable relief."[14] The structures of modern representation become political when they are no longer taken for granted; when either on the level of voice or music or film, their shape is rendered abnormally. This self-focused form of representation not only communicates a social context, but calls attention to the capacity of representation in general, and its own in particular, to reshape and historicize the transcendental givens of everyday experience like time and space.[15]

Brecht was the architect of a radical aesthetic that incorporated the mass media into its basic strategy. Either in his theory or his practice, he was one of the few Marxists to challenge the "bourgeois entertainment industry" on

---

[14] R. G. Davis, "Benjamin, Storytelling and Brecht in the USA," <u>New German Criticism</u>, no. 17 (April 1979), pp. 143-56.

[15] Bertolt Brecht, <u>Brecht on Theatre</u>, trans. John Willet (New York: Hill and Wang, 1957).

its own turf (Benjamin did, too!). The critique the two of them launched against popular culture was more sympathetic than Adorno's. It did not disparage the intelligence or sensibility of mass audiences. Quite the contrary, it clearly envisioned ways in which mass culture's organs and media (e.g., newspapers, film), forms and formats (opera, propaganda), might better arouse them to full and critical cultural participation. Their theories provide the categories for understanding telecommunications' impact on our social and political gestalt today, probably because both men were so sensitive to that horizon that separates the modern from the archaic (storytelling, Chinese acting) in communication.

At the same time, the fusion of modernism and mass production in art has left the Marxist aesthetic debate of the thirties hanging. There is uncertainty about the significance of its central point, realism.[16] On the one hand, the vulgarization of the avant-garde has anachronized Adorno's "strategy of hibernation" (Habermas). The disciples of the men and women Adorno pinned his hopes upon are living in Hollywood, writing scores for mass-circulated films; or living in New York and painting abstract expressionist paintings for corporate office buildings. This cooptation might appear to validate Benjamin and Brecht retroactively. After all, if mechanical reproduction makes art

---

[16] Terry Eagleton, "German Aesthetic Duels," New Left Review, no. 107 (January 1978), pp. 21-38.

that is suitable to the times, then even high art will succumb to its logic. The problem is today's popular culture is widely perceived to be of an irredeemably poor quality. Its inveterate fetishism would appear to discredit their positive outlook regarding the technology.

Into this void has rushed structuralism. Since the 1960s, structuralism has restored the formal analysis to the study of the artifacts of mass culture that Adorno and Horkheimer earlier abandoned. At the same time, in focusing exclusively on the text or on the material components of language (the "signifier"), structuralism gives short shrift to political and historical actuality (at least it has been so accused).[17] Ironically, the very feature of its method that opens mass culture up to sophisticated compositional analysis is what makes this accusation possible. Its exclusive emphasis on signification, which asks, "Does it signify?" not, apropos of Adorno, "Does it signify as well as something else?" demotes real events, political or otherwise, to the insignificant status of 'referential illusion'.

The purpose of this work is to investigate the connections between aesthetics and ideology within the sphere of popular culture as developed in the historical and contemporary writings of Walter Benjamin, Bertolt Brecht and Theodor Adorno, on the one hand, and the latter-day

---

[17]Jonathan Culler, <u>Ferdinand de Saussure</u> (New York: Penguin Books, 1977).

Structuralists, Umberto Eco and Roland Barthes, on the other. The most paradigmatic writings of the above authors have been chosen in order to crystallize their individual positions as well as their differences with, and similarities to, each other.

The aim of this study is to cross-fertilize these two traditions in a way that has never been done before. This cross-fertilization allows for each to become the remedy for the deficiencies of the other. The influence of the Marxist corpus on the Structuralist one will be to situate the latter in political praxis. Conversely, a structural approach to the Marxist writings will make explicit the often implied formalism of their thought. This formalism in turn will show their polemics in a common perspective, a perspective that will furnish a new foundation for a contemporary political theory of mass culture.

I propose that such a theory of mass culture be based on the following theses:

--A vital and intimate connection does, in fact, exist between art and politics. A major portion of the Frankfurt School's writings in exile concern themselves with this nexus.

--Aesthetics should be connected to politics via form rather than content. Since political ideology presumes a specifically structured way of seeing the world, art should restructure. Progressive art threatens the continual success of class-biased communication by laying bare its groundplan. It unravels the matrix in which the thoughts and perceptions we take most for granted are embedded.

--The way art proceeds against ideology is, like ideology itself, historically determined. Technology and social organization influence the way we structure the world. Therefore, aesthetic form, although not as obviously historical as message or content, is a barometer of outside social pressures. There is no necessarily historical information contained in a picture of a wheatfield. Whether or not this picture is a photograph, a realistic painting or a highly abstract one is, however, expressive of the forces and relations of production of a given society.

--Art and language that are revolutionary have three fundamental formal traits. They are:

Fragmentism. Twelve-tone composition does not bring the music to consummation as did the classical symphony. As lives are arrested and incomplete under capitalism, thus should remain art. By the same token, mechanical reproduction's obsessive repetition--consider the recurrent verses of the hit tune--offers neither the sinuosity of the symphony nor the symbolic protest of the fragment. Nonetheless, Benjamin emphasized the flash of the partial cinematic image and Brecht, the theatrical moment over the evolution of plot.

Multiplicity. Meaning, be it literary, visual or sonorous, must be multitudinous and contradictory if it is not to be ideological. The multi-angled, superimposed profiles of the filmed face; the counterpossibilities behind the Brechtian gest; the variants of the magazine caption (Barthes), and the heterogeneity of the dissonant chord all express this ideal. A single image with varied perspectives has manifold meanings.

<u>Ambiguity</u>. No one perspective is valued over the others. One vacillates between possibilities, entertains opposites, plays with paradox. (In dissonance, the three tones collide and coexist.) Ideology excludes contrary perspectives. Radical art balances between them. Ambiguity assumes multiplicity, as multiplicity implies ambiguity.

<u>System</u>. Adorno's negative treatment of Stravinsky delineates his main departure from Brecht and Benjamin. Stravinsky's fragmentation (his snippets of jazz, for example) was slapdash. Schoenberg's ensued from an all-important "constancy of form." Adorno was not interested in anarchy or in taking images out of a context for the shock value. He believed the latter were what Stravinsky and mass culture were all about and deplored them. Schoenberg's system integrated the listener (within himself, not with society). Stravinsky's unreasoned music turned listeners into passive, unthinking consumers. Adorno opposed noncerebral art. This unyielding opposition was the reason for his forays against mass culture and Benjamin's ideas of the same.

Chapter I

WALTER BENJAMIN: THE CHANGING OF THE SUPERSTRUCTURE

Two essays form the subject of this chapter. "The Work of Art in the Age of Mechanical Reproduction" was written in 1936 for the Institute for Social Research, who published it in New York in the organization's journal, the Zeitschrift fur Sozialforschung. The second, "The Author as Producer," was an address delivered in 1934 to the Paris Institute for the Study of Fascism. Together, they lay the foundation for the remainder of this work by analyzing the physical structure of popular art and linking it to political advocacy.

I have taken the liberty of reversing their chronological order in my exposition, since Benjamin's analysis of how the intellectual/artist can best promote socialism is premised on the primacy of technological considerations. The more focused analysis of mechanical reproduction, which was published later, provides a context for the first, programmatic argument. In addition, there is something in the nature of Benjamin's text that seems to invite such liberties. Benjamin once said that the true writer is never relieved to finish what he is working on so that he can return to a normal existence. His true metier is the fragment, which permits him to remain caught within "the magic circle" of the unfinished work.[1] Perhaps this conviction is responsible for the feeling one reader experienced from reading his essays that a segment of any one of them could be transplanted to any other without disturbing the integrity of either.[2] Benjamin's penchant for fragmentation must be appreciated, especially by those readers who expect his ideas to progress step by step in a straight line.

"The Work of Art in the Age of Mechanical Reproduction" is a seminal essay. It puts popular culture on the map by singling out what makes it structurally and socially distinct from other kinds of high art. By focusing on the technology's transformation of the methods of production and reception of art, Benjamin creates a set of standards by which to judge popular culture on its own terms. Before it, writers on aesthetics considered mass culture a deficient version of classical art. After it, even those who disagreed with its proposals had to take popular culture seriously--at least on the level of intellectual argument. In this essay, Benjamin brings to light many of popular

---

[1] Quoted in T. D. Adorno, The Philosophy of Modern Music, trans. Anne G. Mitchell and Wesley V. Lomster (New York: Seabury Press, 1973), p. 121.

[2] Susan Buck-Morss, "Walter Benjamin II," New Left Review, No. 109 (September 1982), p. 95.

culture's implications for political life, implications that are more fully drawn out in the essay following.

It was Benjamin's thesis in "The Work of Art in the Age of Mechanical Reproduction" that just as the infrastructure of capitalist society is constantly transformed by technological development, so is the superstructure, the difference being that the pace of change is slower in the superstructure.[3] The recent technology of mechanical reproduction has inaugurated a new epoch in sense perception analogous to that brought on by the printing press. Benjamin's models were radio and newspaper, film and photography, because they were the most advanced instances of the trends he was describing. Since the processes he distinguishes, however, persist into the present, our examples will not be limited to what was available to Benjamin. On the contrary, the aim of this chapter is to chart Benjamin's way of linking mass culture to politics, <u>and</u> to prove its contemporaneity. It starts to answer the question of how aesthetics affect ideology within mass culture.

Benjamin's brief survey of past techniques of mechanical reproduction (coinage, woodcutting, lithography) should not detain us as much as his central trope: the aura. The aura of a work of art is "its presence in time and space, its unique existence at the place where it happens to be."[4]

---

[3] Benjamin, "The Work of Art," pp. 217-18.

[4] Ibid., p. 220.

Authenticity is one meaning of aura. Mechanical reproduction's indiscriminate replication of the art object, its dispersion of it into "a plurality of copies," dispensed with authenticity as a measure of value or even a meaningful concept in art. It did this by destroying the work's temporal and spatial individuality, by causing it to lose its context and 'place on line' in the continuum of tradition.

No longer moored to a specific physical location, the work of art could be activated through its image in places having nothing to do with its origins, usual environs or customary social uses and receptions. The rise of mass culture thus coincided with the propagation of countless simulacra of precious works of art as well as their free-for-all dissemination to the public. Benjamin calls mechanical reproduction's influence on classical culture "a far-reaching liquidation."[5] This liquidation or "catharsis" came about as a result of culture coming to be composed of freefloating images that could be concatenated without regard for received meanings or past affinities. The technique of radical juxtapositioning, as practiced both by the early twentieth-century Surrealism and modern-day advertising, is ultimately the exploitation of a license inherent in culture's material construction. To differentiate the new art from the irreplicable art of the Classical era, Benjamin invents the concept of the aura.

---

[5]Ibid., p. 222.

Why would this changeover interest anyone other than an art historian? The answer depends upon the way the Frankfurt School conceptualized the social and political function of art in the nineteenth century. The notion of "affirmative art," first outlined by Marcuse one year after the publication of Benjamin's essay, contended that art under early capitalism compensated for the paucity of opportunities for individual expression in the economic and political realms.[6] Under capitalism, individual political expression is tolerated only in the abstract--through voting. Economically, relations of production are utilitarian and uniformizing. Aesthetic experience provided a unique space of freedom and self-communion for the lone bourgeois, and, in that sense, made authentic individuality possible. Classical art was "autonomous" because it was based on the laws of symmetry rather than the marketplace. It did not answer to the division of labor, competition and the overall meniality of existence. The very fact that, in its transcendental vision, it had escaped the hegemonic reality made this art the embodiment of a critique of prevailing social conditions. "Art, since it became autonomous, has preserved the utopia that evaporated from religion."[7]

---

[6] Herbert Marcuse, "The Affirmative Character of Culture," in *Negations: Essays in Critical Theory*, trans. Jeremy J. Shapiro (Boston: Beacon Press, 1968).

[7] Max Horkheimer, "Art and Mass Culture," in *Critical Theory*, trans. Mathew J. O'Connell, et al. (New York: Herder and Herder, 1972), p. 275.

Nonetheless, the independence of "affirmative culture" was ambiguous. It survived because of the polarization between everyday life and liberation. Elitist art was divorced from the practical world. Its emancipatory values were practiced in a ghetto of the imagination. They were vicarious. Marcuse argued that the forces of production under advanced capitalism had developed to the point where this need no longer be the case. The freedom symbolized by art could serve as a prototype for all of social relations. If it did not, if aesthetic 'truths' remained unintegrated with the material sphere, then art would remain a handmaiden of false consciousness, of ideology. One Benjamin critic sized up this contradictory position well:

> No small cause for lamentation is the affirmative-apologetic position culture comes to occupy with the advent of the nineteenth century l'art pour l'art, i.e., art as the ersatz, sublimated sphere where the values denied in material life per se can be harmlessly realized, and more importantly, enjoyed. And in addition to this pointedly a-social 'high' art, the century of bourgeois counterrevolution witnesses a proliferation of entertainment literature. . . . In essence, once bourgeois society in its conservative phase demands an art that is uncontroversial, innocuous, and untroublesome to its conscience, the entirety of traditional culture is also placed in a problematical light: for it then becomes, unwittingly, a possible ally in the bourgeois veneration and worship of culture in order to defuse its potentially damning powers of social criticism.[8]

---

[8] Richard Wolin, "From Messianism to Materialism: The Later Aesthetics of Walter Benjamin," New German Critique, no. 22 (December 1981), p. 29.

Benjamin's theory of the aura was significant in its own context, because, one, it appraised the changing culture of advanced capitalism responsible for leaving the above situation behind; and two, it revealed the transition to be the death knell of a certain characteristic bourgeois experience of ideology.

Benjamin emphasizes the historical connections between art and religion. After art ceased to be an actual adjunct to the religious ceremony, i.e., after it became autonomous, it continued to be revered as if it were sacred. From the Renaissance on, Benjamin informs us, this attitude of devotion was secularized in the bourgeois cult of beauty. The destruction of artistic authenticity, first, through the burgeoning reproduction of auratic art; and next, through the institutionalization of the "work of art designed for reproducibility," thus, constituted a profanation, a denaturing, of the quasi-religious article.[9]

Let us back up for a moment: the "work of art designed for reproducibility" is one that derives, from its inaugural stages, from mechanical copying procedures. It is a reproduction in the first instance. For example, prints from a photographic negative are all absolutely identical. The question of authenticity, of originality, cannot be entertained with regard to them. Which print was developed first in the laboratory is wholly without meaning

---

[9] Benjamin, "The Work of Art," pp. 223-24.

for its intrinsic value. The point Benjamin is making is that the bourgeois was bound to comport himself differently before such a work. Traditional postures of deference were untenable before an innate duplicate, a tawdry xerox. Hence, the loss of aura, which was brought on by technological development, corresponded to the loss of a whole gamut of class-bound emotional and psychological experiences springing from the identification of art and ritual.

Horkheimer and Adorno were ambivalent about what they agreed was this new regime in art. They conceded that there was something progressive in the irreverence now shown to art. At the same time, mechanization had the effect of extending the influence of the market to the one area of life that had been immune to it. Mass art was thoroughly commodified, "administered." It could offer no deliverance from the routinizing pressures exerted by the rest of the institutions of society. It certainly was not the dialectical overcoming of art's earlier remoteness from reality envisaged by Marcuse.[10]

Benjamin chose to see in the levelling of the content and value of the art object brought about by mechanical reproduction (after all, all images are composed of celluloid, the same cheap substance) not banalization, but democratization. The truth of Adorno's and Horkheimer's

---

[10] T. D. Adorno, "Adorno to Benjamin," in Bloch et al., Aesthetics and Politics, p. 124.

repudiation of mass art lay in the latter's parallel with the incorporation of the individual into mass society. There is a structural equivalence between the anonymity of the individual in the crowd and the indifference of the art object built for reproduction. The atoms in the group are as indistinguishable from each other as the photographic prints from the negative. The physical structure of mass art mirrored the structure of emerging social institutions. Adorno and Horkheimer computed the implications of this development solely in terms of the losses incurred to traditional art. Benjamin, on the other hand, saw it as a vehicle of identity formation for the masses. Increasingly, he found the masses

> . . . overcoming the uniqueness of every reality by accepting its reproduction. Every day the urge grows stronger to get hold of an object at very close range by way of its likeness, its reproduction. Unmistakably, reproduction as offered by picture magazines and newsreels differs from the image seen by the unarmed eye. Uniqueness and permanence are as closely linked in the latter as are transitoriness and reproducibility in the former. To pry an object from its shell, to destroy its aura, is the mark of a perception whose 'sense of the universal equality of things' has increased to such a degree that it extracts it even from a unique object by means of reproduction. Thus is manifested in the field of perception what in the theoretical sphere is noticeable in the increasing importance of statistics. The adjustment of reality to the masses and of the masses to reality is a process of unlimited scope, as much for thinking as for perception.[11]

It is not just that the mass public begins viewing the 'same old reality' differently. Rather, the objective reality

---

[11] Benjamin, "The Work of Art," p. 223.

begins to be organized in conformance with a rising mode and apparatus for reckoning reality. Much of modern art has been devoted to exploring the implications of the fact that the idiom of modern self-awareness is similitude.[12] Here Benjamin is saying that our readiness to understand a given aspect of reality through its multiple likenesses is part of the same turn of mind that makes statistics the device for analyzing, planning and predicting that it is in today's society. Technological art is linked in its structural foundations to a new grasp of the world about us, a grasp that has its own special limits and capacities. The former can teach us what those limits and capacities are, or remind us what they are when we forget.

Separating art from ritual shifted the former to another practice, according to Benjamin--to politics. This should not be confused with the idea of politicizing art, for it is the practice that becomes political, not the subject matter. As art loses its religiosity, it simultaneously

---

[12] In the 1980 Werner Fassbinder film, "Lili Marlene," about the eponymous hit song of World War II, a conversation occurs between the songstress and a high-ranking Nazi officer. The two of them marvel repeatedly over the news they have received that "6 million" soldiers on the Eastern Front tune in to the pop tune nightly. The number "6 million" is repeated back and forth, between them several times. Because of the subsequent historical significance given to that particular figure, the effect for contemporary audiences is to superimpose statistics, song reproduction (the hit song is played annoyingly frequently throughout the film), and mass homicide in a single symbol. The inconceivability of the number "6 million," despite its rhetorical and symbolic investment, implies the same connection Benjamin is about to make between mechanical reproduction and the aestheticization of war.

loses its innerness, its depth. It becomes exclusively concerned with outward appearances. "Exhibition value" replaces cult value. The value of mechanical art comes to lie in pure display and sensual enjoyment rather than spiritual salvation. Art thereafter lends itself to the mundane. In particular, politicians and product manufacturers use it to ingratiate themselves and their products with the public.

Henceforward, art must be located in the commodity form, even though it occurs there as a mere support to the selling of products.[13] Its commercialism deterred Adorno and Horkheimer from calling this new type of cultural production "art." Benjamin, on the other hand, appreciated that art and goods and information had begun to be intertwined in a partnership that changed all of them. All art is ultimately advertisement, publicity, in the age of mechanical reproduction (indeed, there may come a time when we do not even recognize art for what it is, Benjamin prognosticates), just as all advertisement has aesthetic production values.

Politics is drawn into this showiness, this reign of exhibition value, since the politician must make effective use of the equipment no less than the screen actor: "Though their tasks may be different, the change affects equally the actor and the ruler. The trend is toward establishing controllable and transferrable skills under certain social conditions. This results in a new selection before the

---

[13]Benjamin, "The Work of Art," p. 225.

equipment before which the star and the dictator emerge victorious."[14] Once art is injected into politics, moreover, the possibilities for subverting ideology grow. For if art can be introduced into the broadcasting of ordinary information, then the radical techniques that change consciousness can be taken out of the museums and galleries and applied there as well.

The political significance of the mechanical reproduction of art goes beyond this blanketing aestheticization of everything that swerves into public view. It arises out of the documentary realism of the photographic and filmic images. With mechanical reproduction, art acquires testimonial power, an ability to bear witness. Benjamin uses the term "evidence" to describe the unpopulated cityscapes of an early urban landscape photographer. He also says that as this power of bearing witness became practicable, verbal cues were instituted in publishing to circumscribe it. Magazine editors started putting captions and "signposts" without and within their pictures. The accuracy of their written explanations was less important than the control the latter gave them over the pictures' presumed significance. The finality of their wording inhibited the reader from making up his own explanation for the picture, from indulging in "freefloating contemplation" before the news image.[15]

-----

[14]Ibid., p. 247.

[15]Ibid., p. 226. Atget was the photographer.

In other words, the authoritativeness of the graphic record, which stems from its perfect documentation of the subject it reproduces, acquired, as its correlate, an authoritarianism from the arbitrary text that necessarily attended and continues to attend it.

Once again, we find ourselves on a limb as to the significance of the now ubiquitous caption. Benjamin does not help us, but his reticence is nothing unusual. Adorno complained once of his friend's theoretical "asceticism," his habit of making an important observation, then breezily going on to another point without further remark.[16] Benjamin abstains from further comment on the importance of the fact that the reader's and filmgoer's interpretations are now controlled beforehand, their reveries outlawed, the former, as already stated, by captions, and the latter, by the succession of frames that predetermines the meaning of each one in the series. (An exception must be made in the latter case for avant-garde films, where there is no storyline and the frames stand by themselves as hermetic, free-standing images.)

We may seek an answer, and, if not an answer at least an interesting parallel, in the more recent work of the semiologist, Roland Barthes. Barthes maintains that the relation between the photographic "analogy" and its verbal fix in today's mass culture is one of _ideology_. His argument develops Benjamin's in the following way: the text of

---

[16]Adorno, "Adorno to Benjamin," p. 128.

a photographic "message," according to Barthes, "connotes" the image, or, conditions its definition. Previously, if we were to consider, let us say, an encyclopedia, hand-drawings illustrated groups of words. They supplied their denotation. One returned to the text after the imagistic reprieve, knowing it had been connoted, that its meaning had been supplemented by the requisite illustration.[17]

The reverse is presently the case. The text of a photograph determines and guides the reception of the image, while appearing to be merely disclosing an obvious content. The words seem to lend the objective reality already present in the photograph a verbal format, and that is all. But because the photographic image is a one-hundred percent reproduction of the reality it cites, a "message without a code" as Barthes calls it, then the text is actually "loading" it in the act of tagging on a verbal auxiliary. Burdening the picture with its own predispositions, it appears to be seconding, in an unproblematically factual way, a self-evident image:

> Formerly, there was reduction from text to image; today, there is amplification from the one to the other. The connotation is now experienced only as the natural resonance of the fundamental denotation constituted by the photographic analogy and we are confronted with a typical process of the naturalization of the cultural.[18]

---

[17]Roland Barthes, "The Photographic Message," in Image-Music-Text, trans. Stephen Heath (New York: Hill and Wang, 1977), pp. 224-26.

[18]Ibid., p. 26.

Marx speaks of how capitalist ideology treats historical phenomena as though they were effects of nature. Social casualties are in this way imbued with a sense of inevitability, of trans-human causality. Their bogus naturalness innures the society to them, making root change unthinkable. Barthes says that this is what the photograph is doing for the written advice placed alongside it. The verbal message appears to be attesting a natural fact, whereas, in reality, it is adumbrating it with its own hidden cultural prejudices.[19]

What is interesting from the Benjaminian point of view is that it is mechanical reproduction that introduces into art the need for some kind of logocentric regulation of the iconic image. It is as though once tradition recedes in importance, and art becomes a document of reality that anybody can read, including the masses (which is not the case with a painting), then and only then does it become necessary to obtrude a linguistic meaning (a "culture") onto the apparent reality (the "nature"). As soon as meaning becomes accessible to the masses, elites monopolize it. That is why it makes sense for Barthes to be speaking of ideology as a relationship between image and word.

Barthes adds another explanation to the notion that verbal language is ideological in the way it affects the reportage of the photograph. He, thus, provides a further

---

[19]Ibid.

elucidation of Benjamin's briskly made point. Images give rise to multiple interpretations, Barthes explains. Their precise meaning is never definitive or univocal. They are intrinsically ambiguous. The text, he continues, delegitimates all but one of the potential readings. It, in a sense, pronounces a verdict on the image's content without the cooperation or interlocution of the reader:

> . . . the text directs the reader through the signifieds of the image, causing him to avoid some and receive others; by means of often subtle dis-patching, it remote-controls him towards a meaning chosen in advance. . . . The text is indeed . . . society's right of inspection over the image. . . . The text has thus a repressive value and we can see that it is at this level that the morality and ideology of a society are above all invested.[20]

In both of the above examples, ideology is defined in terms of a false atonement--first, between the word and the image, which are wrongly collapsed into each other by way of The Word, and second, between the protean interpretations of the image, which are sacrificed to the one definition secured ahead of time. Verbal language puts the viewer's imagination in a vise.

Benjamin also regards ideology as that which diminishes the input of the ordinary reader or spectator by forcing a monolithic meaning upon him. As with Barthes, there is also an intimate tie for him between authority or authorship and polyvalency. For instance, one of the features

---

[20] Ibid., p. 40.

of film that is counter-ideological is optical <u>test</u>. Test is the ability, such as that made possible by the camera, to maintain diverse, concurrent perspectives of a single object.[21] It is important, because it catholicizes thinking. The camera assumes many vantage points with respect to the actor. The audience in a film is on a par with the camera lens. It is thus active and aggressive in its relation to the object projected.

Test shifts control away from the artist and the artwork, toward the beholder. The actor in a film reacts to the shooting camera, while the audience moves in closer, assumes different angles, and shifts about. It holds before its eyes a whole sequence of positions ("takes") of the organic object, breaking it up the way a mobile camera does. Benjamin reminds us that the unity of the film is the end result of a mechanical stick-and-paste production process: parts of a scene may be shot weeks apart and spliced together in the studio to form a continuous whole; the director may finagle an actor into a certain response (e.g., fright) in order to get an adventitious shot of a facial expression the script calls for; that which takes hours to shoot on location unfolds instantaneously on screen. These examples demonstrate, not only that art has become too disjointed, too factitious, to any longer be considered a 'beautiful semblance' of reality; but that the spectator's perception

---

[21] Benjamin, "The Work of Art," pp. 228-30.

has followed suit. It has become montagist, fragmented. The audience's handling of the natural object has become impious as a matter of course. The authority and initiative of composition, thus, fall, not only to the director, but vicariously to the mass audience, who "produce" the image in concert with him.

It was said earlier that ideology is defined as that which endows the given with an unquestionable obviousness. The habits of perception inculcated in the modern audience by mechanical test help the latter resist this obviousness. They condition the citizen to be more skeptical toward received truths. The latter do not seem as stolid or stationary as they did before. By giving the spectator the power and inclination to shift perspectives at will, the camera strengthens his will against political tyranny and the tyranny of meaning. The simultaneity of viewpoints undermines orthodoxy by purely formal means.

The mechanization of perception welcomes the trading of positions between bystander and expert, reader and author, passer-by and "movie extra." In a culture based on total realism, that is, mechanical reproduction, all citizens are within ear- and eyeshot of the appliances of art. We see recently, for example, how video has catapulated some very nondescript situations onto the plane of art. We also see how television has turned rock and roll audiences into performers. In donning outlandish costumes, the spectators make themselves into the spectacle. They dress for the camera and attract the spotlight. They transgress their assigned roles. The prerogative of meaning falls to them. This lack of submission is what Benjamin claimed characterized modern audiences. It bodes well for political change.

In modern culture, audiences have the tendency to become their own objects of attention. Benjamin says--and returns to this theme more than once--every person in today's society possesses "a legitimate claim to be reproduced."[22] The worker's claim derives from his mastery of a microscopic portion of the work process. The latter, in its division of labor, parallels the camera's mechanical parcellation of reality and thereby suits it as subject matter. (The reason for this is that the division that mechanical reproduction subjects the object to, in order to get it right for the camera, preexists it in the case of labor. The rhythms and motions of the manufacturing and recording processes dovetail.) The worker's knowledge of his job establishes his "access to authorship." In capitalist countries, Benjamin says, this entitlement to have oneself reproduced is abrogated "through illusion promoting spectacles and dubious speculations."[23]

Nonetheless, a cinema unapologetic about reflecting life just as it was, about exposing the affinities between

---

[22] Ibid., pp. 231-32.

[23] Ibid., p. 232.

work and culture, could at the time of Benjamin's writing be glimpsed in the Soviet Union. Benjamin points enthusiastically to Russian films in which the actors were really workers portraying themselves in their daily occupational activities. The specialist sharing the details of his livelihood, allowing us into his bailiwick, constituted for Benjamin a model use of the technology.

The point is popular culture allows everyday concerns to become the raw material of culture. It enables the ordinary person to ratify the truth of his experience by elevating it to the level of art. In this regard, it represents a revolutionary improvement over high art, which disdained all but exalted themes.

The contemporary Polish filmmaker, Andrei Wadja, eulogized this earlier cinematic genre in his 1981 film, Man of Marble. In so doing, he brought out many of the tensions in Benjamin's argument. The film is about a young Polish graduate student in filmmaking who discovers some old films in the state archives. She sets out to track down the whole story behind their subject, a worker-hero from the 1950s. The material she has found has been censored, so the story is only partially available to her. As she places the rest of the facts together by studying the clips and interviewing people, the political humbug of the Communist government is exposed as and through the escalating duplicity of these documentary films. Her research quickly becomes an allegory for how reality is sieved by instruments of proof like the camera, as well as how the misshapen results can be repaired through de-construction.

The gap between appearance and reality opened up and exploited by the Stalinist leadership exemplified the problematic nature of the technology in relation to politics. Both in the worker's heroization and his eventual fall from grace, the camera had been made a ventriloquist for the government. The truth had not been dissembled in a positive sense. Rather, the meaning of what was permitted to be shown on screen was incomplete. It was a function of what had been left out, the "off the record," which the student pursues with the help of the films' "clues." Thus, the political enemies of the state were made to confess to trumped up charges of treason on camera. When the hero failed to follow his "stage directions" and instead asserted his innocence, a hand was placed in front of the camera before it was abruptly shut off. Indeed, the attention of the camera and tape recorder is what displaced actual history to the "behind-the-scenes."

The initial promise of mechanical reproduction, Wardja seems to be saying, has only been brought to partial fruition. The technology does have the capacity to report the strict truth. We benefit from having the record of past events it preserves for us, and the truth emerges, like a long buried shard, almost in spite of itself. Nonetheless, as long as we live in a capitalist society, this capacity will be abused. The realism of the technology will trap us in illusion. Under present circumstances, the subject of art cannot be history itself. It must be the methods by which modern forms of representation falsify and delete history. Technological art must be art about technology: how it divorces us from reality in the name of complete disclosure, and how it can be used to restore us to the same.

The next film in the sequence, <u>Man of Iron</u>, seems to redeem Benjamin's positive vision of technological art. Narrating a story around the victory of the Polish Workers' Union, it apocalyptically interpolates actual news footage of the events into the plot. Lech Walesa plays himself when the story calls for the labor leader's inclusion as a character. Thus, fact and fiction are put on an equal par, as though to say, echoing Benjamin, that in revolutionary circumstances, realistic art would simply function as a recordkeeping or repository for actual historical occurrences. The authenticity of life would insure the authenticity of its recreation, the healing of the wound between reality and appearance. In this second redemptive film, too, Wardja returns to the (auratic) Polish folk song in the score in place of the sophisticated, synthesized, electronic rock and roll of <u>Man of Marble</u>. The restoration of fact to fiction --which coincides with the workers' victory over ideology --calls for a similar restoration of a more archaic, whole art object. The workers' coming to power is celebrated by

Wardja with an auratic respect for real events and intact culture.[24]

Benjamin would agree that the verism of mechanical reproduction has a socialist component. The exactitude of mechanical reproduction, its high fidelity, ensues from a step-by-step manufacturing process. It is not attributable to individual vision or skill of execution. It bears no traces of inspiration, of individual genius. It stands in the same relation to the auratic art object as the industrial commodity to the artisan's handicraft.

The mimetic representation, which emerges from the studio and editing rooms, looks absolutely innocent of the artificial dismantling and aggregative procedures, for example, the separation and synchronization of auditory and visual input, which have produced its lifelikeness. The more atomized the process of manufacture becomes, the less does evidence of the equipment survive into the final image. Its accuracy is what makes mechanical reproduction superior to non-mechanical arts, such as painting. The latter approximates. The former engineers the image rather than creates it through the filter of individual personality. Benjamin goes so far as to say that this reliable rendering of reality is ". . . what one is entitled to ask from a work of art."[25] And it is here that he is often accused of

---

[24] Man of Marble (1981) d. Andrei Wardja; Man of Iron (1982) d. Andrei Wardja.

[25] Benjamin, "The Work of Art," p. 234.

having overestimated the profundity of the equipment.

Adorno pointed out to Benjamin that the tricks and gimmicks of Hollywood production imbue the image with commodity values, despite its assumed objectivity.[26] He disagreed that the realism of mass culture promoted clearer social vision, which is really the gist of what Benjamin is saying by equating technological precision with increasing control over reality on the part of the spectator. Recent trends in mass culture bear both men out. Adorno was correct in that the machinations of aesthetic realism are used to mystify audiences. The dials in the recording studio may be turned in such a way as to maximize the clarity of the singing vocals--or, in such a way as to make a thirty year old man sound like a teenager. Sound tracking may sensitize us to the world around us, or package the "sounds of a summer day" for an iced-tea commercial. I believe these were the kind of hypocrisies Adorno was warning against.

Benjamin, for his part, believed that it was up to the revolutionary intellectual to school himself in the fine points of the use of technology in order to instruct audiences in the matter of their manipulation. A radical technique would be one that restored technology to the function of information (even if it is information about the pitfalls of technology), from those of seduction and

---

[26]Adorno, "Adorno to Benjamin," p. 124.

titillation. (Hence, recent movements in popular music increased the static of records well above technologically available standards of clarity and clearness in order to exemplify, through negation, how the most incisive reproduction can be a means to deception in our consumer society. To some, clarity is an arguable good.)

What we are seeing now is that the realism of which modern mass culture is uniquely capable, the realism touted by Benjamin, is itself coming under attack. The practice of resorting to intentionally crude, substandard imagery is an aesthetic-political statement in the sense envisioned by Benjamin, even though it appears, at first, to contradict him with its anti-realism. It is, however, consistent with the revelatory role he confided to the political artist, because scrapping technological advances in a commercial setting implies a sophisticated understanding of the technology and how to neutralize it. Crudeness is achieved by means of the selfsame technology that attains the higher standard, and from which this regressive treatment is a flagrant retreat. In essence, it takes technology to negate its own negation. Thus, Benjamin's positive evaluation of the technology has been vindicated, albeit in a larger sense, the original, early twentieth-century Marxist controversy over realism, of which the essay under discussion is a cornerstone, has never been finally resolved. Questions about authenticity and technology still obtain.

It is fair to say that, while Benjamin concurred with Adorno that technology can mislead, he, also, rated very high the expertise of the mass audience. Mechanical reproduction puts the masses in the cultural driver's seat by adapting art to the peculiar viewing needs of large groups. It facilitates the "simultaneous collective enjoyment" of art by the masses. Edification and pleasure are reconciled in the film. The masses hail the very same innovations that they distrusted when the avant-garde tried them. (His example: the limited acceptance of Dadism versus the popularity of the grotesque film.) This union of "the critical and receptive attitudes of the public" makes the art of mechanical reproduction the only socially relevant art. Its relevance consists in the fact that it alone can bring new ideas to the majority of people. The masses are intelligent when consuming this brand of art, dull witted when they have to depend on critics to interpret art they cannot respond to spontaneously. Benjamin considered an intellectually self-reliant audience a buffer against ideology.

It is the physical circumstances surrounding the consumption of mechanical culture that pry the masses open to new developments in art--and to new developments in social theory, disguised as entertainment. Such circumstances permit people to interact throughout the duration of the piece and harness the energy of the jostling crowd: ". . . individual reactions are predetermined by the mass audience response they are about to produce. . . . they control each other."[27] A medium such as painting is made in private and needs to be encountered the same way. Its solemnity inhibits mass participation. The greater public is not without taste or educability, as critics of mass culture have always averred. It simply prefers the kind of art that will allow for such chain reactions. The mechanical art form is already segmented by the process that produces it. Audience interventions do nothing more to disrupt it. The clapping, stomping and shouting at a movie theatre or electronic rock concert are random and contagious. They insert themselves into the performance without damaging its integrity or presentability. By contrast, at an opera, audience reaction is controlled by protocol.

Ultimately, a new kind of relationship between individuals and society is kindled out of this less monadic, less encapsulated response to culture. Art acquires a much wider social impact than it ever had in the past. The less art caters to small groups, the more it will serve as a medium of social change. Since individuals respond more directly and confidently to what is put before them when they can cue each other, art now can be used to explode the ballast of institutionalized opinion.

There is another feature of mechanical reproduction which makes art accessible to the masses. Through its method of manufacture discussed above, mechanical reproduction

---

[27] Benjamin, "The Work of Art," p. 234.

extends and enlarges our faculties of acoustical and optical perception. Benjamin compares our growth in this area with Freud's <u>Psychopathology of Everyday Life</u>. The latter isolated and projected within the purview of everyday knowledge quasi-intentional acts such as slips of the tongue, memory lapses and incorrect recollections. Before Freud, people were impervious to these "accidents." After him, they were pointedly aware of their existence.

Mechanical reproduction similarly heightens our consciousness of the physical environment. The camera's operations--its "lowerings and liftings, its interruptions and isolations, its extensions and accelerations, its enlargements and reductions"--are instrumental in this regard.[28] They bring out minutiae in the shapes of things, which are invisible to the naked eye. People eventually begin to see the way the camera does. They become more astute about how things are made--including their own impressions. Like a video recorder, they subject all social life to instant replay.

Thus, mechanical art not only interfaces with politics and the market, it does the same with science. In focusing on a "screened behavior item" such as the thigh muscle of an Olympic runner, for example, we derive our aesthetic pleasure from being able to watch the anatomical workings of the human body with lancing insight. The realism of popular art is then actually a hyper-realism that leads to a quantum increase in people's knowledge of the world about them. It makes the

---

[28]Ibid., pp. 235-36.

world "naturally" more vivid, detailed and analyzable to them. A world that presents itself to man in machine-like terms is one that offers itself to change through human activity.

One of Benjamin's key insights here is to connect art in mass society to the physical needs of large viewing audiences. The reader is asked to consider the mammoth spaces that harbor the masses' reception to art. The art shown in these spaces must have an amplitude and kineticism that can only be gotten from a highly technological infrastructure. If one of going to be in a stadium with 50,000 others, for physiological reasons alone, one is likely to prefer the accentuated shrillness of an electric guitar to the subdued sound of an acoustic, no matter what one's taste in music. Conversely, the audience's adaptation to the special intensities of mechanical art has repercussions on future artistic content, which invites more and more mediation by the apparatus.

Materially, the suitability of art for public showing is an unprecedented historical achievement. It is a result of three interwoven trends--the disintegration of the auratic object, the technological manufacture of realism and the physiological transformation of sense perception. Benjamin and Brecht considered these trends irreversible. They were firmly on the side of popular culture for that reason. No matter what they thought of its present manifestations, they knew that it alone provided the prerequisites for mass involvement in culture. It alone provided the machinery of enlightenment, the microphone of political reason. Their writings reflect a need to find a method for communicating political insights with and through this machinery.

Aside from heightening our vision, mechanical reproduction affects our proportions of time and space. There is no hint of an accusation of escapism when Benjamin describes how technology enlarges the area over which our minds and bodies exercise jurisdiction. His excitement is palpable:

> Our taverns and our metropolitan streets, our offices and our factories appeared to have us locked up hopelessly. Then came the film and burst this prison-world asunder, by the dynamite of a tenth of a second, so that now, in the midst of its far-flung debris, we calmly and adventurously go traveling. With the close-up, space extends with slow motion, movement is extended. The enlargement of a snapshot does not simply render what in any case was visible though unclear; it reveals entirely new structural formations of the subject. Evidentially, a different nature opens itself to the camera than opens to the naked eye--if only because an unconsciously penetrated space is substituted for a space consciously explored.[29]

What audience could withstand thus pushing back of frontiers? Benjamin provides an unusual rebuttal to the mass society theorists. As we shall see, for the latter no special spaces of adventure were dilated by the camera; no interstitial freedoms flourished at the outskirts of our work life. They are and do for Benjamin, suggesting that art provides the masses with a trapdoor out of political

---

[29]Ibid., p. 237.

indoctrination and social conformity. A highly powered personal vision can compensate for the claustrophobia of life under late capitalism.

We see here how very contradictory are mechanical reproduction's contribution to culture. On the one hand, it mechanizes the process of cultural production. It dismembers it, step by step, and distributes the several tasks of composition among disparate individuals, each concerned with his own isolated input. The producer (i.e. the actor) is even separated from the object of his labor (i.e., Benjamin's example of editing in shots without and actor's control or foreknowledge). All of this spells alienation in Marxian terms, and justifies Adorno's and other political scientists' jaundice toward mass culture.

On the other hand, the new art fortifies individuality on a novel basis: it sharpens the ordinary person's perceptual faculties; it gains him access to virgin universes, thus extending his control over his immediate environment and his scope of action; it conjures an image of reality so true, the most plainspoken individual gets to arbitrate its veracity. Benjamin never leads us out of these antinomies. However, his treatment is slanted enough in the direction of the positive to cause Adorno to accuse him of romanticism.[30]

Benjamin bowed to this criticism by occasionally

---

[30] Adorno, "Adorno to Benjamin," p. 123.

qualifying his mostly favorable reading of mechanical reproduction. Such qualifications notwithstanding, Benjamin believed that this new kind of culture, and this one alone, gave man the means to deal with the quotidian hazards of the modern world. Its practical assistance to contemporary men and women came from its "ballistics"--the shock effects produced on the spectator by bombarding him with swift changes in "place and focus."[31] (Today, we would have to include in the description the invasive, voluminous, ambient sound of stereophony.)

The kineticism of film takes out of the onlooker's hands the choice to suspend himself before a great work of art, to ponder it, to "abandon himself to his associations."[32] The space to which mechanical reproduction initiates us is redolent of the street, with its darting traffic and booming noises. Both embody the experience of distraction. Mechanically reproduced art violently upsets the spectator's senses, where the old art tranquilized and enraptured him. The divided concentration the whizbang of competing sense detections produces describes the contemporary habit of mind. Distraction, or the mental bouncing from stimulus to stimulus, the being ripped apart from images we might like to fasten onto, characterizes cultural reception in general.

---

[31]Benjamin, "The Work of Art," p. 234.

[32]Ibid., pp. 238-39.

For Benjamin, the barrage that is now art does not warrant removing the latter from serious consideration as culture. Earlier, distraction was thought to be the direct opposite effect of what art was supposed to produce: passage into another, more serene, world. The film screen riddles the spectator with dashes of light and sound. Images assail his senses, pull him this way and that. Great art was supposed to enfold the spectator in peace and quiet. Bourgeois art critics refused to classify cinema with the high arts, because of the way it violated personal space. But Benjamin felt their categories, like the middle-class art they explained, were obsolete. He refused to dismiss film on the grounds that its instability of focus, its roller-coaster-like distraction, put it in the category of light entertainment. He has recourse to the pre-history of mass art to explain his rethinking of critical categories.

The earliest sign of a transition in modes of cultural reception was the post-World War I avant-garde movement of Dadaism. Dada achieved the collision effects of technology, the vertigo, conceptually rather than through electronification. It shocked, outraged and threw audiences off balance. For example, at its first public exhibition, a toilet seat was suspended over the entrance. Benjamin says, "In the decline of middle-class society, contemplation became a school for asocial behavior; it was countered by distraction as a variant of social conduct."[33] In other words, Dada was a self-consciously political pummelling of bourgeois sanctimoniousness in the face of art.

But film was not self-consciously moral--it was purely physical in its effects. Its simulation of the buffets and the dangers of the city street has just been mentioned. In addition, its "industrialization of perception" (as one contemporary Benjamin critic has dubbed it) offered the worker a sensual equivalent of the machine.[34] Distraction became the tool with which man began to make sense out of his experience in the modern world. With it, he was and is able to objectify the physical turmoil he is placed under, by industrial living. That way he can control it. Moreover, avant-garde art, which was seen by Adorno as the epitome of cultural resistance against capitalism, was seen by Benjamin as a mere transition phase to mechanical art. The attacks on bourgeois values in the first kind of art ceased to be overtly expressed. Instead, they were absorbed into the physical dynamics of the second kind, where they remain to this day.

The distraction of mass culture, however, is more than a rehearsal for the physical abuse of industrial society. Benjamin claims that art presents solutions to certain perceptual tasks confronting populaces at given points in history. The new mode of reception film engenders--that of a

---

[33] Ibid., p. 238.

[34] Buck-Morss, "Walter Benjamin II," p. 94.

"collectivity in a state of distraction"--is the paradigm of a learning process. The ordinary person in today's world is confronted with extraordinary amounts of information necessary to the conducting of his life. Distraction is a technique that permits him to handle these torrents of information. Through mass art, the group soaks up ideas that one by one the individual members would probably be unable or unmotivated to master.

The principle behind this feat of knowledge acquisition is habit. The habitual intake of information occurs at the peripheries of audience awareness, aslant attention. That is why, today, when a complex concept is introduced into popular usage, it is done through several media simultaneously. A fragmented consciousness, addressed on many sensory levels, can sustain more data than a wholly attentive one that has information linearly schooled into it. Thus, according to Benjamin, popular art was then ushering in a perceptual mode that would eventually serve as a new public pedagogy.[35]

Adorno questioned this part of Benjamin's essay unsympathetically, claiming that distraction was only necessary as a relief from alienated, diurnal labor. He thought it small compensation for the day's woes, one which bound the worker all the more securely to the status quo, by shatter- his ego so that he was unable to deal with the causes of

---

[35] Benjamin, "The Work of Art," pp. 239-40.

his boredom. (You will recall that Horkheimer felt that
the contemplation of the artistic masterpiece was the single
opportunity the individual had to be alone with himself and
stake out an identity under capitalist conditions.) Distraction in culture was a sign of the worker's flagging concentration at the end of the workshift. It tolled his dehumaniza-
tion, not his hope.[36] This objection was based on a
partial reading of Benjamin's explanation of distraction as a
characteristic cultural experience. The fuller gloss was
given by Benjamin in the digression on architecture.

Architecture, Benjamin says, is the prototype of the
masses' relation to art. There are two ways of "appropriat-
ing" a building. One is optically, e.g., the lone tourist
gazing steadfastly in front of a famous landmark. The other
is tactually, as occurs through use. "Tactile appropriation
is accomplished not so much by attention as by habit." The
first type of exposure forms a one-dimensional, visual
impression in the front of the spectator's mind. The second
type occurs over a period of time and leaves behind a
kinesthetic memory, that is, a physical orientation, in the
user. It sets him in a behavioral groove, gives him body
knowledge. Like tying one's shoelaces, the person internalizes the building, performs within a relationship to it,
without the full supervision of his mind. Benjamin wants us
to take this group rote (for many people use the building at

---

[36]Adorno, "Adorno to Benjamin," p. 123.

once) as an educational model:

> This mode of appropriation, developed with reference to architecture, in certain circumstances acquires a canonical value. For the tasks which face the human apparatus of perception at the turning points of history cannot be solved by optical means alone, that is, by contemplation alone. They are mastered gradually by habit under the guidance of tactile appropriation.[37]

The contemporary example of television news may amplify what Benjamin means by "canonical value." During a typical network newscast, many facts are communicated to the viewer in a prescribed amount of time. The facts are condensed into short clips, which are alternated with steady speed. (Interspersed within changes of headlines and topics are changes in camera angle and physical location.) The time apportioned to each news item is fairly even. The passage from one burst of data to the next is quick and predictable. The import or complexity of each report may require more time to be explained than that invariably allotted them. Yet, if Benjamin is correct, an inordinate amount of information can be processed by this "frame-flipping" procedure--that is, by suppressing direct attention and delivering broken up bits of information, obliquely, incidentally, repetitiously. Even the most static type of broadcast, the Presidential address, makes use of this dynamic principle in the motions of the camera, which create a sense of movement and disconnection even though nothing

---

[37]Benjamin, "The Work of Art," pp. 239-40.

is happening within the frame to justify it.

It is important to realize that, just as the film makes objects real to its viewers without exposing them as integral forms for prolonged, meditative inspection, advertisements, with their "insistent jerky nearness" and upbeat tempo do likewise.[38] The techniques of distraction--rapid-fire timing, optical zoom--are indifferent to the uses to which they are finally put. Divorcing art from ritual and transferring it to the showcase of exhibition made it amoral. We are dealing with a base "sense perception that has been changed by technology," an appetite (and capacity) for spectacular sights and raucous sounds, which seeks gratification in art. Furthermore, this art is now thoroughly integrated with and mobilized by all sectors of society, from the political to the private. Different things may be being said, but the way they are said remains the same.

Here is a structural understanding of mechanical art apart from its capitalist uses and its propagandistic ones. The use of radio made by totalitarian leaders to insinuate their presence into the far corners of private life was actually a throwback as far as the post-auratic nature of the medium was concerned. Mechanical reproduction takes the magic or charisma out of representation. Fascism tries to put it back in. So does capitalism by purposefully confusing

---

[38] Walter Benjamin, "One-Way Street," in Reflections, trans. Edmund Jephcott (New York: Harcourt Brace Jovanovich, Inc., 1978), pp. 85-6.

the aesthetic realism of the technology with that of the advertising claims of its commodities. It displaces the one onto the other. Either way, the technology has gone awry. Adorno, as we shall see, believed it was bound to happen. He attempts to show that mechanical art sets people up for totaritarianism. Benjamin, on the contrary, separates the theory of the technology from the practice of it under capitalism. All along, he has been arguing the social potential of popular culture. At the end of the essay, he reverses himself by saying that this potential has been mangled.

Benjamin adopts the Marxist understanding of war as the sole means the capitalist system has of employing at full tilt the tremendous forces of production it is responsible for unleashing. In a parallel manner, the technological grandiosity of war satisfies the enlarged appetite for sensual stimulus of generations reared on mechanical reproduction. (This was before the era of computer toys.) ". . . [Mankind's] self-alienation has reached such a degree that it can experience its own destruction as an aesthetic pleasure of the first order."[39] Indeed, just as capitalism proliferates needless commodities in order to perpetuate itself, its techniques of packaging and promotion grow increasingly extravagant, from the aesthetic standpoint, in relation to the mediocre goods they are called upon to sell.

---

[39] Benjamin, "The Work of Art," p. 242.

Only war is cinematic enough to justify consumer society's mechanical hoopla.

At first, the fact that mechanical art was purely external in meaning, that it had lost its numinous aspect, came as a liberation from the ideological pretensions of bourgeois art. Ultimately, however, it led and leads to a divorce between appearance and substance. Our new vistas enable us to look at war in a purely detached way, as aesthetic extravanza: war for war's sake. Not only has politics adapted to the formal demands of mechanical reproduction, because it has had to, but at least part of the success of Fascism is attributable to the new aesthetic. Like a Hollywood production number, formations of goosestepping armies make dynamic use of the camera. The camera captures their awesome symmetry. Adorno later admonished that the mechanical decomposition of the natural object caused psychic dissociation in its viewers, leading, in turn, to fascism. Benjamin claims rather that the strength of mechanical reproduction (its ability to cut through the mystique of objects) is also the source of its weaknesses (draining the object of all reality outside its image).

Benjamin does not only value ambiguity in the subject matter he is writing about, he welcomes it into the very format of his argument. His assessment of mechanical reproduction is Janus-faced. One of its profiles smiles on the mechanical apparatus's pellucid mirroring of reality, in particular, the masses and their ant-like movements when seen from a bird's-eye perspective. The parade, the "monster rally," the sports event and war all can be envisioned better with a camera than without one. No one individual can attain the same comprehensive perspective as the machine. Thus, the mechanical image, by acquainting the masses with their full breadth, introduce them to a collective identity. Through it, the masses descry themselves as a social force.

The opposite profile of this Janus visage, however, frowns upon the way this identity has taken shape under capitalism. The masses' alienation manifests itself as an ideal consumption of their own reproductions, of the spectacle of destruction. Benjamin ends his essay on this conundrum. Speaking of war, he says, "This is the situation of politics which Fascism is rendering aesthetic. Communism responds by politicizing art."[40]

In the light of these two unacceptable alternatives --unacceptable because they either mobilize the equipment toward perverse ends, or retard it for reasons of ideological purity--the unspoken question is whether a truly progressive, modern mass art exists, or has the potential to exist. It is to this problem that Benjamin turns his attention in "The Author as Producer."

In the New York-Paris correspondence between Adorno and Benjamin, we read Adorno chiding Benjamin for either

---

[40] Ibid.

being too Marxist, or not Marxist enough.[41] In "The Author as Producer," Benjamin answers his criticism by reformulating, in his own way, Adorno's notion of "autonomous art" and the politically effective choices available to "the poet." In it, he tries to cut a middle path between Adorno's aloofness from mass culture and riotous commercialism.

Benjamin starts out in this essay by examining the idea of autonomy in relation to the bourgeois writer. He finds a paradox in the following: If the writer writes for publication, he is selling his talents to the bourgeois entertainment industry, knowingly or unknowingly. If, on the other hand, he eschews collaboration with capitalist class interests, as is the case with the politically conscious bourgeois writer, one of his only other choices is to work on behalf of the working class cause. He is then choosing "to side with the proletariat." Either way, Benjamin points out, the writer gives up his independence. "Tendentiousness" in art (later, the term "committed" will be in vogue) is no less a sign of being answerable to a third party than is mass circulation. The only way around this neither/nor situation is to somehow link political correctness with literary quality and <u>vice versa</u>. The artist's finesse with the material, the full exercise of his formal skills and creativity, should be the measure of his work's independence and political

---

[41] Adorno, "Adorno to Benjamin," p. 130.

significance. The best art should be the best politics.[42]

Benjamin then says that a dialectical approach to the problem of political art will first of all rid itself of cliched assumptions about genre. The novel, the book or the commercially mountable work of art presents obstacles to our thinking about, and recognition of, incipient forms of expression, forms which, being incident to political praxis, have not yet gelled into specifiable categories. (Recall that in "The Work of Art in the Age of Mechanical Reproduction" a similar point is made to the effect that art is no longer what has a frame hung around it and is suspended on the walls of museums. To wit, part of the problem in talking about revolutionary art is first determining what one is talking about.) Once we stop taking conventional forms as our measure, we can resist the more obvious content with the question, "Where does the work fit within the 'literary relations of production' of its time?"[43]

The technique of the work is the key factor to be considered in answering this question. ("In bringing up technique," Benjamin says, "I have named the concept that makes literary problems directly accessible to a social, and therefore a materialist analysis.")[44] This is in keeping

---

[42]Benjamin, "The Author as Producer," in <u>Reflections</u>, pp. 220-21.

[43]Ibid., p. 222.

[44]Ibid.

with his formalist approach to the art of mechanical reproduction. Here, however, the author focuses on the attack points of the artist/intellectual toward the aesthetic-industrial complex.

In "The Author as Producer," Benjamin suggests there is a way to convert the problems which verge on art (its acceptance, distribution, commercialization, and so forth) into art. Progressive art should not only attempt to change attitudes. It should seek to change institutions. Technique influences perception, and it also influences the way the cultural establishment is run. There is a strategy forthcoming for the production of a certain kind of art that causes the profit-making mechanism of capitalist culture to grind its wheels. Something about the fragment, for example, makes it harder to merchandise than the novel. What is new here is a broadening of the basic structural argument we have been following so far, to include the external situation in which art finds itself. Technique can make aesthetic problems "accessible to materialist analysis" only in the age of mechanical reproduction. The latter's equipment-intensive art acquires a technical and social malleability and social relevance lacking in the individually oriented art of the past. The positive side of popular art being cheaply made is that the means to make it oneself and thereby reinterpret its functions are readily available.

Benjamin begins with the example of what he calls
the "operating," as opposed to the "informing," writer of
Russian descent, Sergei Tretiakov. Significantly, he conceives of Tretiakov's activism in the area of agricultural
collectivism--calling mass meetings, creating wall posters,
collecting money for tractors, editing newspapers--as artistic
ventures.[45] Benjamin interpreting these acts as art
accords with what he said earlier about nascent forms. It
also assumes that in any revolutionary situation, the formal
properties of representation are inseparable from their
practical functions, or which is to say the same thing,
revolutionary movements call forth revolutionary modes of
expression and are augmented by them, in turn. Ideas must
have aesthetically redeeming qualities.

In his 1929 essay on Surrealism, Benjamin anticipates
both of these essays by calling for a utilitarian art that
does not sacrifice excellence. The intelligentsia, according to him, has failed to make contact with the proletariat
because it has persistently attempted to do so contemplatively. Popular culture, as we saw before, sweeps people up
into it. It has outmoded the contemplative stance. No
longer can writers and artists conduct the cultural
class struggle from their own mounts. Speaking of the "image
sphere" as the living language that is born and incubated
in political action, he asserts, "In reality it is far less

---

[45]Ibid., p. 223.

a matter of making the artist or bourgeois origin into a master of 'proletarian art' than of deploying him, even at the expense of his artistic activity, at important points in this sphere of imagery."[46] The bourgeois "artist" may have to upset the comfortable relationship he has with cultural institutions in order to be so deployed.

Returning to "The Author as Producer," Benjamin maintains that the relationship of the intellectual to the masses is no longer a tutorial one because of the tendency of mechanical culture to promote the average person to the position of expert. The transformation of the ordinary person into an expert flows from the audience's involvement in mechanical art. (When Adorno looked at mass culture, he saw millions of people going to the same concerts, viewing the same movies, idolizing the same stars. Benjamin saw the interviews with the fans who, part of the crowd or not, felt fully qualified to speak about their idols as though they knew them firsthand and enjoyed a special relationship with them.) The Soviet practice of casting workers in the role of themselves (producer as author) best demonstrated how the average person could be made into a licensed spokesman. In Russia, Benjamin noticed, social labor was becoming linked to elocution.

---

[46]Walter Benjamin, "Surrealism," in Reflections, p. 191. Here Benjamin implies that it is only through redemptive language that reality may be fully known: "The collective is a body, too, and the physis that is being organized for it in technology can, through all its political and factual reality, only be produced in that image sphere to which profane illumination initiates us."

Being published was beginning to become a matter of "polytechnic education" rather than highly refined writing skills. Benjamin's contention is that when workers have their own part in the dialogue that is culture, traditional lesions between production and ideological advocacy close up.

For Benjamin, the newspaper was the organ of such a verbal empowerment in capitalist countries, albeit one "owned by the opposition." What it indicated to him was the inverse: The intellectual must struggle around the process of production as an intellectual. He cannot affect the balance of power simply by espousing attitudes, even sympathetic ones, toward the proletariat. He must somehow engage the problem of technique if he is to be more than an "ideological" patron." In other words, his contribution to the class struggle should go beyond donating an idea or opinion.[47]

When Benjamin says that the author must struggle as a producer, he means he must effect change in the "literary relations of production." He borrows a neologism from Brecht to describe such a generic intervention: <u>Umfunktionierung</u>, meaning "functional transformation."[48] An <u>Umfunktionierung</u> is a technologically rooted structural innovation that rehabilitates proven genres. Such inventions change the formal relationships of traditional works. They alter

---

[48]Benjamin, "Author as Producer," pp. 225-26.

[48]Ibid., p. 228.

the rules of the language game, not to jolt audiences, but to build new and sounder networks between technology, the work, and social consumption.

Of course, the danger here is that because the genuinely transformative work tampers with deeply couched structures of representation, it may appear, on first exposure, to be gratuitously meaningless. Chaos is good when it leads to a rethinking of normal responses. It is bad when it is copied as an end in itself, because it has become the symbol of the avant-garde. As Adorno put it so well in 1962, "Such works drift to the brink of indifference, degenerate insensibly into mere hobbies, into idle repetition of formulas now abandoned in other art-forms, into trivial patterns. . . . Formal structures which challenge the lying positivism of meaning can easily slide into a different sort of vacuity, positivistic arrangements, empty juggling with elements."[49]

Benjamin is quite clear about the fact that a <u>functional transformation</u> catalyzes audiences in new, socially important ways. For example, at the time of Benjamin's writing, the increasing rationalization of the methods of musical manufacture or reproduction was polarizing the specialized producer/technician and the amateur, increasingly listless listener. It was also creating a gap between studio and stage work, for what could be performed in an auditorium was pallid compared to what could be synthesized in the

---

[49] Adorno, "Commitment," p. 191.

engineering room. As these gaps began to widen, conservative forms like the commercial orchestral concert continued as before, doing nothing to counteract the increasing isolation of the audience from the art-making process.

Then, according to Benjamin, along came Brecht and Eisler and introduced political lyrics into what had formerly been the preserve of the musical instrument. Their didactic play form used words and accompaniment to engage the audience, to stay their drift. The aesthetic and political were thus put in tandem with one another (as were technique and content). Through verbal involvement, audiences were taught not to expect a canned product. The performance ceased to be a faint substitute for the record. Responsive reading exposed the audience to politics through the content of the lyrics. All in all, the introduction of the word into a form that had previously disallowed it put the technology at the disposal of the audience (through amplification and the like) rather than employing it in such a way as to exclude them. At the same time, says Benjamin, the literary quality of The Measures Taken (the didactic play he used as his example) was not lowered at all by being used to pioneer changes in conventional patterns of consumption and thus patterns of exposure to new ideas and experiences.

Benjamin is quick to add that the "mere supplying" of a productive apparatus goes against its re-organizing. It is often the revolutionary sounding works, works which are vehement in their anti-capitalist sentiment, which prove absorbable by the system. ". . . a considerable proportion of left-wing literature possessed no other function than to wring from the political situation a continuous stream of novel effects for the entertainment of the public."[50] These works may trumpet deviant values, but they have not challenged the structural chassis of the genre that subsumes them. No matter how much they harangue their opposition to capitalism, the substance of that opposition remains vacuously rhetorical, perhaps even titillating, as long as the indentations of the works match some part of the jigsaw of the cultural marketplace. A truly transformative work uncovers the limits the marketable genre imposes on the public by not acceding to them unthinkingly. Of course, since Benjamin is sketching a political approach to popular cuture, he does not attempt to prove this point, so much as illustrate it with examples.

Benjamin's own examples of functional transformation are elucidating. Dadaism flouted the elitism of high art by pasting onto the canvas of the painting--cigarette butts, tickets, spools of cotton--the waste matter of everyday life, which was thought to have no rightful place in culture. Pioneering work in photomontage politicized the book cover. As time elapsed, the deliberate barbarisms of these two movements were refined and stylized into salable motifs. The

---

[50] Benjamin, "The Author as Producer," p. 231.

result of their treatment and processing was that the "tenement block" and the "refuge heap" went from being troublesome, effective effigies momentarily suspended in the public mind's eye, to commodifiable images eclipsed and reified by "style." Photography retreated from its investigatory function to that of apologia: "For it has succeeded in transforming even abject poverty, by recording it in a fashionably perfect manner, into an object of enjoyment."[51] The function of photography continued, as before, to be the registration of the world, only it now did this in order to beautify it "from within." Uttering something through aesthetic formula may well make it acceptable. Structures may deaden people to the impact of a certain image or, on the contrary, make them alive to it in a new way. This is the distinction political artists must bear in mind if they are to push the issues they want into the social foreground.

What happened to Dada and photography came as a result of artists supplying rather than revamping the apparatus. To do the latter, in this case, would have meant overcoming the rift between word and image (as Brecht and Eisler did for language and music). The photographer must be able to rationalize his image in such a way that "wrenches it from modish commerce" and realizes its "revolutionary useful value." Reciprocally, the writer must learn to recognize and articulate the technical processes that coopt

---

[51]Ibid., p. 229.

photography. Technical insight into the workings of mass communications is an important political tool. The artist and intellectual, along with other "productive forces," need each other's expertise to understand their own neutralization. They also depend upon others to commandeer new technological developments for the creation of a more humanistic art. (Today, we can see just the opposite. Unemployed actors and artists, glad to find a job, pioneer applications of the new video technology for major corporations. Through their short-sighted, obliging efforts, cable art's exchange value is being charted, its use value, nipped in the bud.)

In this non-logocentric alliance, the writer translates and superintends what is happening in the other image-systems. Yet the intellectual cannot be effective in his orchestrating role without transcending another of the divisions his discipline subjects him to: that of the academic versus the popularizer.[52] Good popularization reflects a knowledge of how symbols, technologies and professional pressures work together at <u>both</u> the level of form and content. In other words, the intellectual must not only expose the relationship between language and power, he must illustrate it in his own language. His language should body forth the issues under discussion. (Example: if he is talking about the pellets of cinematic images that rain down on moviegoers, together with their social effects, he will communicate the

---

[52] Ibid., p. 230.

idea with a staccato style rather than professional jargon. On the other hand, fashionable language unsupported by insight is a concession to commercialism.) Although these requirements sound formidable, such decompartmentalization actually accelerates during and as part of the class struggle.

The first major point that has been made so far is that the immanent form of a work of art often serves a specific commercial need. Destroying the latter's appearance of aesthetic necessity reveals its underlying commercial function. It is plain to see that fragmentation makes of a commercial culture filled with rigidly defined genres a playground for the independent creator. The amateur becomes a composer in his own right, making art out of the several elements that have been set free from their normally prescribed uses.

The second point is that the radical intellectual cannot deal exclusively with content. He must also understand and cope with the problem of form. Either he learns to scramble the codes of the culture industry, or he bows to them. A difficult implication arises here having to do with the relationship between the aesthetic presentation of ideas and their truth value. Benjamin, Adorno and Barthes all agree that such a relationship exists. Benjamin's writing is sometimes so fragmentary, one feels that to do an academic treatise on it is to be somehow unfaithful to its basic intent. Barthes, in his autobiography, criticized an analytical work on television for being "insufficiently protected aesthetically." Adorno once saw fit to discredit Lukacs' ideas on the basis of his writing style. Yet on another occasion, he implies that the mistakes behind Benjamin's distraction theory are covered up by its "shock-like seduction." Perhaps it is fair to say that what distinguishes these writers is their struggle to find that elusive balance between form and content, a struggle that never ended with a final policy on where the balance lay.[53]

Art which does not have an "organizing function" in the system of production, continues Benjamin, is liable to convert, not only the objects of, but the struggle against penury into an object of "contemplative amusement." Luridness, for example, may masquerade as political message. Scholars may mummify revolutionary art by writing about it, instead of finding new ways to put its principles into practice. The artist who shifts the foundation of a genre however can share his structural insights with other artists. His creative ploys can prompt other professionals to confound the categories of contemporary publication, and having done so, place "an improved apparatus at their disposal." His political commitment is thus assured. The mandate to teach others should be extended to the non-expert as well. Roles

---

[53]T. D. Adorno, "Reconciliation under Duress," in *Aesthetics and Politics*, p. 154; Roland Barthes, *Roland Barthes by Roland Barthes*, trans. Richard Howard (New York: Hill and Wang, 1977), p. 104.

should be switched around wherever the authority is one-sided. Works of art should be created that galvanize the reader into writing, the consumer into producing, the audience into collaborating.[54] Then will art have been used to change social psychology.

Jurgen Habermas has interpreted this idea in the light of an experience of a group of German workers, which was reported in the literature by Peter Weiss. The workers were exposed to European art during the late 1930s. They incorporated the "objectified mind" of its different legacies into their lives by finding the common denominator between the structure of the art and that of their own environment. They emulated what they saw with rock and stone "edifices" of their own construction. By comparing the skeletons of the museum artifacts with their own, they divined the structured principles operative in their own world. What was important in this transference was not the official history of the traditions they lifted their specimens from, and for which they had little understanding, but the fact that they could view them apart from an overall context and intuit much from them as individual fragments. Thus, says Habermas, the goal of the revolutionary-critic-pedagogue is to free culture from the stranglehold of academics and critics in order to position it properly for the working classes.[55]

---

[54]Benjamin, "The Author as Producer," p. 233.

[55]Jurgen Habermas, "Modernity vs. Post-Modernity," New German Critique, no. 22 (December 1981), p. 12. Reference is to Peter Weiss, The Aesthetics of Resistance.

Benjamin's ideal of the architectonic political artist is Bertolt Brecht. Brecht's innovations were aimed at the then current state of commercial theatre. Much as today, the theatre had become a welter of machinery, staff and stage effects. Its overdeveloped, costly material infrastructure put the producer-artists in a powerless position to effect change from within the commercial establishment. It was beset by competition for public patronage with radio and film. Its constant efforts to wring reactions out of the audience caused the latter to become oblivious to the fine points of stagecraft. These forces continued to spiral. The theatre was becoming homogenized by what, today, we would call "hype."

Brecht broke out of this vicious circle by putting the theatre on an altogether new footing. By seeking to learn from and enlist the "newer instruments of publication" rather than outdo them, Brecht turned the proscenium into a forum for debate on the issues surrounding media development. He utilized the stage's unique assets--its contact with a live audience, its ability to mix and match electronic and non-electronic media--to create a dramaturgy which had its own indigenous "state of the art" standards. This meant returning to the theatre's simplest elements instead of trying to foster an illusion of reality that had no feasibility for stage. Brecht was more interested in tapping into our perception of the real than in reproducing objective reality. Because of its altered priorities, Brecht's epic theatre succeeded in reorganizing the relationships proper to it: those of the actors and the public; the actors and the director; the performers and the text.[56]

The precise manner in which it accomplished this will be held over for discussion in the following chapter. However, Benjamin cites Brecht's use of montage as an example of how Brecht resuscitated techniques worn out by commercialism. (He changed montage from "a merely modish procedure to a human event.")[57] Although Benjamin's commentary on Brecht echoes what the latter has to say about his own work, it will add to our understanding of Benjamin to learn how he analyzed montage in the context of the author-as-producer.

Brecht used montage to interrupt the actions of the actors in much the way Benjamin speaks of the camera doing. Brecht adapted its mechanistic, start-and-stop procedure for his own purposes: to procure for the onlooker a sense of improbability about, of unsuspected fascination with, ordinary scenes from everyday life. He wished to shake the members of the audience out of their perceptual lethargy toward the events that constituted the building blocks of their lives. He, thus, dispensed with plot, instead freezing the play on scenes of run-of-the-mill behavior. In the schematic incidents he isolated, and not in sweeping events,

---

[56]Benjamin, "The Author as Producer," p. 234.

[57]Ibid., p. 234.

he rooted the "action" of the play. In the most common and transitory gesture, he drew out a whole social choreography.

By putting common behavioral routines under the microscope (never dismissing their idiosyncratism, but playing on it to unfurl their social content), epic theatre invited audiences to study and try out alternatives to them. It, thus, assumed that political change was effected through "reason and practice," and that the key to it lay in these simple slices of social life. Brecht designed this strategy to be like mechanical reproduction with its total recording of environments and its rejection of standards of artworthiness. (To the camera and radio monitor, nothing is too small or too quiet to fail to get picked up and frozen into the perpetuity of representation.) He knew that audiences acculturated to mechanical art were equipped even before coming into contact with epic theatre with an ability to focus on particulars.

Where Brecht also reaped an advantage from cinema was in the audience's readiness to readjust its angle of vision on a scene, time and again, without its getting boring or pointless. As we saw above in Benjamin's explanation of test, occupying several positions relative to a single object shakes up a person's attitude toward it (literally and figuratively). It enables a person to really experience--like a child looking at a moving train from a moving train--the relativity of his positions. Brecht adapted cinematic test in such a way as to concentrate on the cells of human experience rather than the "climaxes."[58] He advanced its usage by restoring in conjunction with it what Benjamin once called "the space in which contemplation moves." That is, he trained it like a magnifying glass on social life, giving people the time and space to digest what they saw. He showed people how to use it to understand their lives better. Rather than exploiting movement and speed for the cheap thrills they could and did give audiences, Brecht turned the perceptual habits motion picture techniques were universalizing to political and pedagogical advantage. As for Lukacs, who frowned on such miniaturistic artistic ambitions, Benjamin seems to anticipate him: "At the center of . . . [Brecht's] experiment is man, present-day man; a reduced man, therefore, chilled in a chilly environment. Since, however, this is the only one we have, it is in our interest to know him."[59]

Benjamin closes his essay by reemphasizing the factual foundations of the author-as-producer's solidarity with the proletariat. In speaking of the artist with revolutionary aspirations, he asks:

> Does he succeed in promoting the socialization of the intellectual means of production? Does he see how he himself can organize the intellectual workers in the production process? Does he

---

[58] Ibid., p. 235.

[59] Ibid., p. 236.

>have proposals for the Umfunktionierung of the
>novel, the drama, the poem?⁶⁰

The accommodations the established artist and writer must make to the institutions that support them are what enfeeble them aesthetically.

This chapter began with Benjamin's discussion of the decline of bourgeois art. It ends with his advice to the activist artist on how to take advantage of the opportunities for political change offered by cultural secularization. The focus up to this point has been on the theory of how technological structures reorient perception. In the following chapter, some of the concrete ways in which art was used to alter people's political worldviews will be explored.

In conclusion, I have only to point out that these last questions posed by Benjamin have a special relevance to the writer, who will be acting as a go-between for his fellow artists. It is the writer who will make possible self-conscious transitions from one emergent form to the next, as well as crossings of the threshhold of the image toward the word, the word toward the image. Which brings us back to the beginning. For this, in fact, is what Benjamin has been doing all along, i.e., by describing the giant, hurling, careening images of advertising. He has been creating a meta-language of post-auratic art.

---

[60] Ibid., p. 235.

Chapter II
BERTOLT BRECHT: THE AUTHOR AS PRODUCER

The relationship between the critic and the artist described by Benjamin in "The Author as Producer" works well to describe the relationship between himself and Brecht. Optimally, the work of art concretely embodies a new act or mode of judgment. The criticism of the work of art then translates into abstract terms the meaning of this passage into another state of consciousness. The experiencing of the innovative work of art leads to an unconscious knowledge, which the critic exposes, as the psychoanalyst, the dream.

Brecht's cultural experiments were the coal from which Benjamin dredged his theoretical diamonds. (Brecht also played critic to his own work, so there is nothing perjorative in this statement.) The following chapter explores the practical dimension of what has been talked about. Brecht used art to agitate people with political mind-sets. He worked with structure rather than exhortation. His dramaturgy used an abstract theory in concrete ways. A discussion of it will thus add flesh to the structural/aesthetic approach to politics taken by this piece.

This chapter relies on Brecht's commentary on his own work rather than literary descriptions of his plays and productions. Although separating theory from practice has its hazards, it also has the advantage of extending the life of certain ideas outside the configurations in which they were originally placed. (This is precisely what Brecht does when he abstracts the idea of the "alienation effect" from ancient Chinese acting.)[1] In addition, Benjamin warned against fetishizing a particular work or author in "The Author as Producer." He advised analyzing the work in terms of the logistics of the entertainment industry. He considered Brecht's plays political, because they related themselves, if wholly negatively, to the bourgeois culture of their time. In 1930, for instance, Brecht wrote of one of his didactic radio plays, "Der Flug der Lindbergs is not intended to be of use to present-day radio but to alter it."[2]

In the meantime, the structures against which Brecht's work asserted itself have evolved. There is thus no need to go into detail about the plays themselves or their historical settings. I have tried to select those ideas that speculate on the relation between form and politics as well as those examples which have the greatest relevance for contemporary mass culture. Example: Brecht

---

[1] Bertolt Brecht, Brecht on Theatre, trans. John Willet (New York: Hill and Wang, 1964), pp. 91-100.

[2] Ibid., p. 32.

tells of a radio show he did in 1939, which was constructed in such a way as to anticipate and evade the effects of wartime jamming. Among other things, rhymeless verse was chosen, because it approximated direct, spontaneous speech. The latter tolerates interruptions far better than the stylized language of poetry. Using it permitted Brecht to stay one step ahead of the censors. Although this strategy was designed to cope with the exigencies of war, it clearly has an interesting application for today if, in place of "jamming," we substitute "advertising" or "commercial interruption."

These parallels between past and present should not surprise us. In fact, part of the goal of this work is to bring them out, to exploit these writers for their generic grasp of mass culture. Mass culture was at its dawn when these men were penning their observations. Their senses had not yet been jaded by electronic "overkill," as ours, predictably, have been. As a result, their writings often take less for granted than contemporary treatments of similar subjects. Just as Benjamin was intellectually susceptible to the impressions made on him by blinking neon lights, Brecht, too, was sensitized by naivete to those first signs of the raid of mass culture into everyday life, to the ambient effects of mechanical reproduction, which today are so common as to sink beneath notice.

Censorship through Form

Brecht echoes Benjamin in saying that the intellectual supplies the raw material for a culture machine that churns out art as merchandise. This machine whittles all ideas down to forms it can accommodate. It controls content:

> Great apparati like the opera, the stage, the press, etc., impose their views as it were incognito. . . . The musicians, writers, and critics . . . by imagining that they have got hold of an apparatus which in fact has got hold of them . . . are supporting an apparatus which is out of their control, which is no longer (as they believe) a means of furthering output but has become an obstacle to output, and specifically, to their own output as it follows a new and original course which the apparatus finds awkward or opposed to its aims.[3]

A word such as "course" is a good one to describe the relationship between art and its institutionalization. According to Brecht, the creative material appears to take shape the way it does out of necessity for what it is expressing. In reality, it is curtailed by the channels it must go through. The channels, the categories, define the direction of new ideas. Without suppressing language and ideas directly, they denature them with formal requirements. They subterraneously dominate thought and expression by routing the work through a maze of formal limits (e.g., the unwritten law that a popular song can be no longer than a couple of minutes).

When an artist or intellectual defies format or is recalcitrant to the "laws of mercantile trade," with their

---

[3]Ibid., p. 34.

tacit (because formal) restrictions on thought and perception, his work falls into immediate neglect. "An opera can only be written for the opera," says Brecht.[4] A new kind of opera that attempts to say things differently is effectively silenced by its loss of access to cultural production and distribution. It is therefore important, according to Brecht, not to try to say new things, but to bring into dialectical conflict the art form and that which the form excludes or makes unthinkable. The commercial dramatist, in opposition to such a view, is content to work within the commercial paradigms. He feels his audience ". . . should not think about to such a project, works within the commerical paradigms rather than loiters between them. He feels his audience ". . . should not think about a subject, but within the confines of the subject." Brecht's art differs from most in that it is always simultaneously a meta-art. His emphasis on "making oneself observer" or investing stage moves with the "gest of showing" makes the actor into a midwife, rather than a tout, of meaning.

Film embroils the spectator's senses by moving around a lot. If the content of the film moves forward in a continuous line, it obscures the role played by the fragmentation of time and space in sustaining his interest. If the storyline itself becomes fragmented, it manifests to the spectator the

---

[4]Ibid., p. 35.

[5]Ibid., p. 44.

nature of his experience. Taking cognizance of the way outside forces are shaping one's reactions is a first step toward preparing reactions that shape outside forces. For this reason, the relationship between form and content is political.

The artist struggles for the room to say what he wants, not for the ideas themselves. For example, a continuing theme in Brecht's writings is the need to maintain a separation between text, music and setting in mixed works of art. The ideas contributed by each are debased by being made to function ". . . as a mere 'feed' to the rest. The process of fusion extends to the spectator who gets thrown into the melting pot too and becomes a passive (suffering) part of the total work of art."[6] Coordinating the different media lulls the spectator into a false sense of harmony. Not doing it pulls him in more than one direction, activating him through conflict.

Background music is a case in point. It is composed to order, usually so that specific emotions, such as happiness, nostalgia, shock and fear, can be triggered in the audience at appropriate moments in the drama. Brecht calls the growing dependence of the audience on the excitement and pacemaking of the soundtrack "sordid intoxication." Indeed, he claims such techniques are addictive. An "addicted" audience gets used to the flaws in the text being smoothed over for it by the music. Its thinking and modes of response grow

---

[6]Ibid., pp. 37-8.

formulaic. Formal barriers, namely the norms that demand that the different media support each other symbiotically, translate into barriers in its thinking.

Brecht's objection to the alloying of text, music, and background was based on a desire to maintain the sobriety of the audience. As Benjamin wrote of Brecht's epic theatre, ". . . interruption is one of the fundamental devices of all structuring. . . . An actor must be able to space his gestures the way a typesetter produces spaced type."[7] This spacing, be it between an actor's gestures or the end of a speech and the beginning of a tune, no matter, the principle of interruption remains the same, insures that the audience will have the time and repose to think and judge. Providing a breather is particularly important in the case of working-class audiences, who, according to Brecht, are not prone to pensivity. It also duplicates the organization of mechanical reproduction, as Benjamin's analogy with the typesetter suggests.

Earlier, Benjamin was reported to have held that the modular construction of the mechanical artwork promotes innovation and audience expertise.[8] Brecht here accounts for why. As discrete entities, the individual media can develop the properties indigenous to their idiom. They can formulate their own approach or "attitude" to the dramatic

---

[7] Walter Benjamin, "What Is Epic Theatre?", in *Illuminations*, p. 151.

[8] See Chapter 1.

problem. A multi-sided development reacts dialectically on the intelligence and sensibility of the audience, who grow accustomed to surprise and ambiguity instead of always having to have their expectations and biases reinforced. The audience is also able to follow more of the ramifications of the music and the like, because it is not under its subliminal influence.

The interconnection in art between technique and politics is found in Brecht in their common goal: the freeing of the audience from illusion so that it can seriously contemplate the issues at hand.

> Once the content becomes, technically speaking, an independent component, to which text, music and setting 'adopt attitudes'; once the illusion is sacrificed to free discussion, and once the spectator, instead of being enabled to have an experience, is forced as it were to cast his vote; then a change has been launched which goes far beyond formal matters and begins for the first time to affect the theatre's social function.[9]

Conventional theatre (today, we may speak in general of all forms of entertainment) seeks to give the audience a 'complete' experience. By gluing the spectator to the story (Brecht spoke of "drugging" the spectator, of making him "punch drunk," or "titillating" him), the production depletes his capacity for action. The frazzled spectator is left with a sense of finality after being held fast to the plot from start to finish. He has no left-over energy to take out with him into the street. All questions have

---

[9] Brecht, Brecht on Theatre, p. 50.

been settled in advance--structurally, by a plot which moves toward and culminates in a prewritten resolution.

This is not so with Brecht's scenes, which, sufficient unto themselves, knock into each other or progress "in spurts," as Benjamin says, "like pictures in a film."[10] Brecht intentionally halts the play's momentum with music, captions and--again Benjamin--"lifeless conventions." He believed that making each moment stand by itself instead of evolving toward a final goal caused audiences to see the depicted events less deterministically. Form fights fatalism.

The disjunction in ordinary theatre does not come between the acts, but between art and life, a disjunction which is maintained, along with the audience's servility, despite the latter's paroxysms within the pen of the auditorium. Brecht's art does not have this satisfying, pacifying closure. Goading the audience into 'adopting an attitude' fosters an involvement which is not supposed to spend itself by the end of the performance. It makes art into a testing ground, a "laboratory" as Benjamin called it, of everyday life in its full assortment of experiences, a forum or "parliament" where plain situations and cropped off parts of situations are dramatically blown up at the precise swivel of their turning points.[11]

That theatrical structure determines behavior, and

---

[10] Benjamin, "What Is Epic Theatre?", p. 153.

[11] Benjamin, "The Author as Producer," p. 231.

that this structure is historical are truisms of Brecht's art. Brecht speaks of the necessity of adapting the auratic arts to an audience perception acclimated to film. Film "sees" the individual from the outside, defines him in terms of his outward actions rather than his inward character, which is where the bourgeois novel locates motivation.[12] (Another way of saying this: film trades on the exhibition value of the human being, the meaning on the surface, the gesture stripped of soul.) The low-technology art form must analyze and adopt the mechanical arts' modalities, because their structures are the ones people are now prepared to think in. "The mechanization of literary production cannot be thrown into reverse," Brecht warns.[13] The mechanical "means of representation" must induce the non-mechanical arts to revise their methods. Spurning commercial art in favor of an idiom such as literature, with its roots in the nineteenth century and remoteness from advertising's kaleidoscopic flashiness, causes elevated art to languish in neglect of "every development in communication." This is the crux of the matter. Do not believe, Brecht is in effect telling the politically progressive artist, that, just because today's cultural commodity is infused with technology, the absence of technology is itself a sign of intelligent revolt.

On the other hand, there is nothing to prevent

---

[12]Brecht, _Brecht on Theatre_, p. 50.

[13]Ibid., p. 47.

archaic techniques from being updated. Brecht, for instance, advocated the theatre becoming "literarized": "Footnotes, and the habit of turning back to check a point, need to be introduced into playwriting."[14] The reader will recall that one of Benjamin's conditions for a revolutionary art was the literarization of the means of production. In the example of the footnote, a verbal device is incorporated into a more mechanized format, because its morphology (that of the pause, the insert, and the review) lends itself to it.

As important as reaching people is the fact that the modern means of representation are uniquely outfitted to portray life under capitalism. Brecht points to the ideological disenchantment of post-auratic art forms like advertising and film. Capitalism

> . . . [takes] given needs on a massive scale, exorcizing them, organizing them and mechanizing them so as to revolutionize everything. Great areas of ideology are destroyed when capitalism concentrates on external action, dissolves everything into processes, abandons the hero as the vehicle for everything and mankind as the measure.[15]

The rationalization of desire may lead to mass marketing of commodities or an unprecedented opportunity to portray individuals in social terms. When the individual's private feelings become only a minor variation on those of the rest of the society, objective explanations force themselves upon art. Although Adorno never felt that Brecht succeeded in

---

[14] Ibid., p. 44.
[15] Ibid., p. 50.

embodying systemic factors in his stage characters, the idea recalls Benjamin's exoneration of mass culture. When art loses its aura and becomes all veneer, it no longer drowns a person in its intimidating depths.

Device functions in Brecht's epic theatre on several levels at once--aesthetic, pedagogic, political. For instance, a certain text may make an actor want to underline its contradictions for the spectator. The fact that epic theatre does not aim for illusion permits the actor to handle this impulse in a creative way. He can "withdraw" from the sentences by declaiming them a little too loudly. He can use tones that reveal themselves to be the end result of prior deliberation. "Mental processes, e.g., demand quite a different tempo from emotional ones, and cannot necessarily stand the same speeding up," Brecht says, apropos of the fact that there is more to acting than simply making situations believable.[16] Altering the pace and reflection with which a line is delivered, aside from giving the audience time to react, calls attention to the mechanical media (the example of television news in the previous chapter) with their uniform, insistent, controlling beat.[17] In commercial mass culture, the speed with which information is surrendered or the affective proximity of the speaker to the message is not modulated in accordance with the variable demands

---

[16] Ibid., p. 55.

[17] See Chapter I.

of the subject matter. Someone in attendance at a Brecht play is expected to experience the difference and become conscious of how restricted his listening comprehension is most of the time.

With the above example, it becomes possible to visualize the interrelated functions of a single technique--interruption. (1) It effects the denotation of the discourse by ordaining it in a less standard way. (Aesthetically, the actor does not merely assume the lines, he breaks them up with his own cogitation.) (2) It prolongs the attention span of the audience (pedagogic). And (3), it makes theatregoing audiences more savvy about the ways in which commercial media program thought (political).

The aesthetic, pedagogic and political aspects of Brecht's technique derive from the difficulties of depicting the complexities of capitalism to audiences "of the scientific age." Individual psychology can no longer telescope a social order, as it could when world-historical figures were the great catalysts of global events. The task of contemporary theatre, according to Brecht, is to concern itself with the depiction of such general occurrences as housing shortages, the export of pigs and speculation in coffee (they are his examples), without simply espying them through the keyhole of personal biography. Technically advanced methods of communication are indispensable to the fulfillment of this task, for they help explain and streamline the complexity of modern life. Speaking of one of his productions, Brecht illustrates how their use bound together aesthetic, pedagogic and political elements:

> Not only did the background adopt an attitude to the events on stage--by big screens recalling other simultaneous events elsewhere, by projecting documents which confirmed or contradicted what the character said, by concrete and intelligible figures to accompany abstract conversations, by figures and sentences to support mimed transactions whose sense was unclear--but the actors, too, refrained from going over wholly into their role. . . .[18]

One can see from the above example and from previous remarks why Brecht advised that the use of screen projections, maps, even statistical material, be presented at a remove from the dramatic action. There is no way to pretend a mass movement is going on, on stage, without traducing the spectacle of the multitudes. Their sheerly physical power calls for mechanical documentation. The Broadway play *Evita*, which was about the political mobilization of the masses, failed to convince us of their political cogency by representing them as a handful of actors on stage, waving clenched fists. Its manner of representing them depoliticized them, though the subject content was manifestly political. (Compare this to Charlie Chaplin's opening rush-hour scene in *Modern Times*. The energy of people going to work is captured in full force.) In pursuit of realism, reality is belied. In Brecht, the audience's sights are never lowered to the

---

[18] Brecht, *Brecht on Theatre*, p. 71.

level of the protagonist's, as is done in naturalistic plays, and the media are never mobilized in the service of illusion. (The latter would denature them, as their virtue lies in their objectivity.) On the other hand, the individual is not swallowed up by the totality either. The meaning of his plight is always overdetermined by personal and political factors.

The non-naturalistic inclusion of mechanical images in Brecht's plays does more to amplify the micro events of the narrative than if the latter were subordinated to the plot. Sacrificing illusion removes the constraints on the aesthetic deployment of the technology. Realism consists not so much in the seamlessness, the logical coherency, of the tale told, in consummate make-believe, such was Lukac's position, but in the full, creative exploitation of the mechanical instruments of expression. The latter not only communicate information about the outside world (see Benjamin); they are themselves palpable reminders of it. The effect produced by employing such instruments in auratic art may be one of fragmentation. But fragmentation is an important part of social life, in part, because of the role played by these instruments in it.

In this all important way, Brecht differed from Adorno, who wanted to seclude art from technology because of how technological art fared politically and commercially under capitalism. Adorno could not envision that situation changing.[19]

───────

[19]Adorno, The Philosophy of Modern Music.

Brecht, on the other hand, as Benjamin explained it in "The Author as Producer," saw art as the place to explore and stage needed improvements.

At the center of Brecht's aesthetic and the obverse of his rejection of all forms of empathy is something he called the "alienation effect." Brecht coined the neologism --he used the term 'Verfremdung', not the 'Entfremdung' associated with Marx and Hegel--in the middle thirties, after his visit to Moscow. It reflected the influence of the Russian Formalist avant-garde theorist of literature, Shklovsky. The latter defined literature as a "making strange" or "defamiliarization" or "estrangement" of commonplace reality. Brecht's adaptation of the concept gave it explicitly political overtones. Frederic Jameson explains it this way:

> The originality of Brecht's theory was to have cut across the opposition between the social and the metaphysical in a new way, and to throw it into a completely different perspective. For Brecht, the primary distinction is not between things and human reality, not between nature and manufactured products or social institutions, but rather between the static and the dynamic, between that which is perceived as changeless, eternal, having no history, and that which is perceived as altering in time and as being essentially historical in character. . . . The purpose of the Brechtian alienation-effect is therefore a political one in the most thorough-going sense of the word; it is, as Brecht insisted over and over, to make you aware that the objects and institutions you thought to be natural were really only historical: the result of change, they themselves henceforth become changeable.[20]

---

[20] Frederic Jameson, <u>The Prison-House of Language: A Critical Account of Structuralism and Russian Formalism</u> (Princeton: Princeton University Press, 1972), p. 58.

More will be said about the A-effect presently.

The distancing of the alienation effect is produced by another of Brecht's techniques, the social gest. The gest is an attitude or group of attitudes that express the quintessence of an epoch. It is a pose struck that typifies in mime the social and political conditions prevailing in a particular society. Brecht says epic theatre is interested in attitudes people adopt toward one another "wherever they are socio-historically significant." There are also illustrative or expressive gests, which Brecht is not interested in. The mimist who affects joy at eating an ice cream cone is not revealing anything about the state of the society he lives in. The one who caricatures the slump of a tailor at his sewing, however, is. The difference for Brecht is that all labor is social. Its gest reflects a particular society at a particular point in time.

According to Brecht, all emotion can be expressed in a picturesque attitude or posture. When an actor performs the gest, he makes it clear he is soliciting the audience for their attention to, or observation of, what is, to begin with, his observations of another. Often the same gesture is repeated, quoted, either by the same actor in a different circumstance or by a different actor. Benjamin points out that observing the observation or "making gestures quotable" is another technique of interruption. As proof, he reminds us that scholarly quotation breaches the text it is referred from and to. "Epic theatre is by definition a gestic theatre for the more frequently we interrupt someone in the act of acting, the more gestures result."[22] Interruption breeds repetition, but not the mechanized, ideological kind of mass culture--rather, the creative, never-heard-the-same-way-again repetition of the quotation. (Adorno never distinguished between the two.) That is why Benjamin defended Brecht against the charge of plagiarism by not defending him. He explains that Brecht welcomed plagiarism, because it set up a relationship, an intertextuality, between the reproduced gesture and the original. When the same line is repeated, its meaning is transfigured by the sudden acquisition of historical specificity.[23]

A modern day example from popular culture explains how. Two vocal artists perform the same song. The second one, who may come ten or fifteen years later in time, makes pointed deviations, which recall, through their absence, the characteristics of the first or older version. Choosing a more constricted harmonic range for a "cover," as it is called, not only makes a statement about the historical conditions that have anachronized harmonics, but also enable us to hear, for the first time, the harmony of the original, which, until the later version, we were too

---

[22]Benjamin, "What Is Epic Theatre," p. 151.

[23]Walter Benjamin, "Brecht's Characters," New Left Review, no. 123 (September 1980), p. 95.

habituated to, to hear separately at all.

Quotation, by departing slightly but significantly from the original, renews it. A mental comparison is forced upon the listening groups, who, because of their common pool of references, know both songs and are thus in a position to appreciate their disparity. When Jimmy Hendrix quotes "Strangers in the Night" in the midst of a screeching guitar riff, they can recall romance in an age and song of industrial-sized violence, for example, gaining insights into the historical factors that condition their own reactions to language and art. Social context is invoked through a purely formal procedure. The quotation both makes room for and elicits this mental checking.

The purpose of alienating reality through the gest, through the brandishing of representation in some unusual manner, is to prompt us to look afresh at what is thoroughly prosaic; to gain a slant on what makes it knowledge-worthy; to disengage us from our normal readings. Take the person who, in the throes of an intimate relationship, conjures memories of the other when he or she was still barely an acquaintance, and then superimposes this earlier stranger on the person or the present lover. This is what the gest does, only it combats the fatigue of familiarity, not with the enamoring one, but with those facets of our social and political existence that we take for granted. (The sexual analogy is a good one, however, because it validates Brecht's answer to a recurrent criticism that his epic theatre was anti-feeling. Just as the lvoer seeks dispassionate objectivity in the midst of thralldom, so, Brecht argued, do people feel more when they are intelligent about their feelings. The gest, which takes what is to be reported on out of the sphere of the merely imitative, requires that both the representation and its object be thought about.

For Lukacs, the nearness of art to life achieved by literal realism "beguiles" the spectator into "re-experiencing" the objective world and, thus, assuming responsibility for it.[24] The Brechtian gest does not try to evoke recognition through resemblance to real life. It endeavors rather to ventilate sheltered ideas by reformulating them. "Representation . . . has inescapably to reckon with the social gest; as soon as one 'represents' (cuts out, marks off the tableau and so discontinues the overall totality), it must be decided whether the gesture is social or not (when it refers not to a particular society but to Man.)"[25] As Barthes observes, the gest challenges official discourse. The latter characteristically construes reality from a specific vantage-point but camouflages the spot or site from which it speaks. The gest, on the other hand, assures us that all representation is preceded by a choice, governed by a strategem.

---

[24] Georg Lukacs, "On Bertolt Brecht," *New Left Review*, no. 123 (September 1980), p. 95.

[25] Roland Barthes, "Diderot, Brecht, Eisenstein," in *Image, Music, Text*, p. 74.

This technique, as is true of all Brecht's techniques, is deduced from bourgeois communication. The latter dulls us to social events the way the machine disciplines the body of the assembly-line worker into repetition. Witness Benjamin's comment in "The Work of Art" about the desire of the masses to "bring things closer," or their ". . . overcoming the uniqueness of every reality by accepting its reproduction."[26] Benjamin is characteristically ambiguous here. Mechanical reproduction elevates the audience to the status of experts. But it also produces that peculiar insensibility to the reality behind the reproduction that is endemic to the modern era. The world is too accessible to us. We are blinded by our ease of recognition, our facility with analogy. Brecht restores some of the world's mystery in order to make us want to explore it again. "Everyday things are thereby raised above the level of the obvious and automatic."[27]

The incidents that take place in Brecht's plays are treated as unique and historically determined. (These two go together. Only the unique stands in need of a social explanation. What is standard can simply be relegated to its 'more of the same' pigeonhole.) Brecht gives the example of a young girl leaving home to find work in the big city. How should the farewell scene be played between the girl and her family? he asks. If it is assumed that there

---

[26]Benjamin, "The Work of Art," p. 223.

[27]Brecht, <u>Brecht on Theatre</u>, p. 92.

nothing intriguing about the girl leaving home--that it happens every day, that it is natural--then the scene will be played without special emphasis, to set the stage for later events. If the scene is regarded as highly exceptional, on the other hand, many questions will have to be answered before it will be able to be rendered properly: Do all children leave home at this age? Did they always? If not, what has changed? Is independence biological? etc.[28]

The alienation effect can be made sense of by remembering what is happening in the superstructure. Benjamin was aware that mechanical reproduction banalizes art, and also that Adorno and Horkheimer counted such banalization an incalculable loss to culture.[29] But Benjamin believed that mechanical art could sanctify everyday life, which high art could not do. That was its revolutionary strongpoint. Surrealism had linked awareness of ordinary objects to political awakening. From Benjamin's "Surrealism" essay, the following explanation of its philosophy can also explain how popular culture effects a self-cure through the A-effect: "For histrionic or fanatical stress on the mysterious side of the mysterious takes us no further; we penetrate the mystery only to the degree that we recognize it in the everyday world, by virtue of a dialectical optic that perceives

---

[28] Ibid., pp. 97-8.

[29] Horkheimer, "Art and Mass Culture."

the everyday as impenetrable, the impenetrable as everyday."[30] The gest is this "dialectical optic." It cures our political malaise by forcing new life into dead questions about how our lives are run.

In "The Author as Producer," Benjamin suggests that revolutionary art undercut the rules of communication. Epic theatre does this by signifying unconventionally. In addition to what has already been discussed, however, the gest has other features that bear directly on the question of a political art. One is its rejection of empathy. The gest, remember, thwarts identification the way an outside intrusion spoils suspense. What does this rejection imply about contemporary forms of popular art that are empathetic? A remark of Benjamin's sheds some light on the answer. He reminds his readers what it would be like for a German exile to play the part of an SS man in Brecht's "The Private Life of the Master Race." The only reason he could do it would be because he would not be asked to "identify with the murderers of his fellow fighters."[31] Epic theatre does not require the actor to surrender himself to his part. It remains at a dutiful distance from the events and emotions it portrays. Regular theatre does not. It aggresses upon the audience by re-enacting atrocities nobody is really capable of comprehending, let alone identifying with.

---

[30] Benjamin, "What Is Epic Theatre"," pp. 153-4.

[31] Brecht, Brecht on Theatre, p. 95.

A fear of glibness comes through in Benjamin's comment. It would also, no doubt, fuel Brecht's contempt for contemporary television "docu-dramas" like "Roots" and "Holocaust." The actors in these programs react to epic events like World War II with the emotional range typical of a weekly detective series. The techniques of suspense and emotional evocation are the same in both. The events and temporality depicted by them are so foreshortened ("brought closer") in their aesthetic conception, the audience ends up by assimilating their contents into their own narrow worlds rather than respecting their transcendence. Brecht understood that tugging at an audience's emotions destroys its capacity for true indignation. The latter unleashes revolt. Therefore, what appears for all intents and purposes to be an innocent dramatic device is actually an ideological poultice.

The technique of the quotable gesture also encourages another of Benjamin's desiderata in "The Author as Producer"--audience participation. The reason is that the success of an action does not depend on how it squares with a sub-conscious intention. It can be

> . . . corrected by comparison with reality (Is that how an angry man really speaks? Is that how an offended man sits down?) and so from outside, by other people. He acts in such a way that nearly every sentence could be followed by a verdict of the audience and practically every gesture is submitted for the public's approval.[32]

---

[32] Ibid., p. 93.

Gestures can be grappled with by the audience. The issues of acting, formal issues, let out onto the political.

How so? Because human behavior is seen as alterable. The attitude is delivered in such a way as to intimate that under different social and political circumstances, it could have been posed otherwise. Since the actor is not concerned with recreating reality from a literal standpoint, he is free to show the audience the preparation that goes into performing his role. "Among all the possible signs certain particular ones are picked out with careful and visible consideration."[33] (The same is true of the scholarly quotation, is it not? Depending upon the context it is used in, some meanings and not others are plucked from those made possible by the original.) An actor should select those signs that somehow remind the audience of, or point to the signs that have not been chosen. This puts the audience in the jockeying position; it alerts them to the fact that other courses might have been taken, and permits them to project how a change in the objective historical conditions or in the approach to the existent ones might influence the actor's rendition of a given character or circumstance. "The scene is played as a piece of history."[34]

Although each choice brings with it certain entailments--as the mimist maintains perfect consistency within

---

[33] Ibid., p. 86.

[34] Ibid., p. 74.

the borders of his illusion, so must the actor be true to his choices--there are offshoot scenarios. The audience makes them up, in debate with the actor. Unlike, as we say in Chapter 1, the magazine that latches its own meaning onto its photographs, there is here a sense of unfinished business. The artist tempts the audience into contradicting him by giving it an overview of his field of choices. He does not present his version as final or inevitable, thereby begrudging the audience its discursive role. The audience is both treated as and trained to be experts.

Even the "subincidents" or ancillary details of a scene are brought into focus this way. Brecht offers the example of a street-corner crowd listening to the retelling of a recently witnessed car accident. The person demonstrating what happened suddenly gets confused. He is not sure if the yell, "Watch out!" heard just prior to the crash came from someone in the car or on the street. He opens the floor to the onlookers. Was the voice male or female, old or young? The group attempts to resolve the question together. Each person searches his own experience, tests and manipulates the possibilities, and finally draws his own conclusions.

A similar transaction goes on between the actor and the audience in one of Brecht's plays. As the person's voice was isolated in order to pinpoint responsibility for the accident, the facts of the play that will be picked out for fuller scrutiny will be those that lead to social consequences. By the same token, television and film deny this critical role to their audiences by setting in stone (or celluloid) the secondary qualities of a representation, such as the tone of a person's voice. Critical thinking is related to the opportunity to intervene and correct. Through consultation, audiences drill through the social cement of fixed ideas.

The car accident example simply shows how the social de-construction Brecht mounts on stage proceeds spontaneously in real life. It also shows the depth of the respect the audience is held in. The audience is assumed to be the expert. It is treated as, indeed, stimulated to be, reasonable and thinking adults. Mass culture, on the other hand, treats the audience as a suggestible herd, and so the audience reacts in kind.[35] Propaganda feeds on itself. The proper kind of art can train the masses to be less gullible.

In Brecht, representation is always a matter of ostensible choice. The actor makes it quite apparent that, as in the car accident retelling, he is actively comprising an interpretation of the events he is describing. His interpretation, further, has social repercussions for which he is plainly taking responsibility. The audience is not overwhelmed with rhetoric. It can look closely at what is being described, and judge its validity for itself. In effect, it becomes the technicians, the crewmen, of its

---

[35]Ibid., pp. 90-137.

own close-ups, first examining the event from one position, then another. It does not have images foisted upon it, as it does in front of a movie screen. It is not "raped" with emotion, since the actors never convert to the personae they are playing. In other words, Brecht's technique remedies the drawback of film implied by the ever ambiguous Benjamin in his choice of the term "ballistics." It affords the audience the clarity of the "screened behavior item," without, at the same time, shooting images at it so that it does not know what it is seeing.

As for practical examples of the above, any sign system may be gestic, even music. (Suggested ways for achieving the A-effect with music: putting complicated, "advanced" music to common tunes; having the actor score his gestures to vulgar music like the striptease; using music which provokes "predetermined emotions" and directing the actors to play against them.) Synthetic sound effects like street noises were classed as desirable for stage by Brecht, while naturalistic sounds, say, those of well-water splashing as two actors bent over it drawing water, were deemed verboten. In language, Brecht favored irregular rhythms, because they promoted "the gestic way of putting things." (Here he often studied street prosodies like the cry of the newspaper hawker on the streetcorner in order to understand why they carried and stuck in one's mind so effectively.) He believed that jazz projected the polyrhythms of everyday life in the industrial world into music. "The ear is certainly in the course of being physiologically transformed," he said, in defense of modeling his art after such serendipitous art.[36] (For Brecht, the street is the ultimate source and authority for what will go on stage.) Even wording and rhetoric may be more or less gestic. (Brecht suggests as an exercise in alienation translating the literary text into the actor's native dialect.) In addition, anything that shows something to be both itself and not itself simultaneously-- seeing one's mother as somebody else's wife, for example--is said to produce alienation.

Therefore, whether it be something remarkably peculiar portrayed with utmost casualness; or the opposite, a "recurrent, modest and vulgar" action executed as if it stands in need of serious explanation; whether it be different media working against each other, or individual episodes untraversed by any ultimate meaning; whether it be the rejection of "perfect examples," which do not make inconsistency as much a part of life as predictability; a text of the play handed over to the audience with the notes from past rehearsals scribbled in the margins, or, finally, a caption that sets off the stylized acting of the play with the flatness of its literalism--the point is all the same. The technique, of which all of the above are homologous examples, introduces fragmentation, ambiguity and multiplicity into settled ways

---

[36]Ibid., p. 191.

of thinking, with the aim of teaching people how to address themselves to political change. The connection between these three characteristics of language and the broadening of a society's political horizons is metaphorized by Brecht in the following image:

> It is the same as when an irrigation expert looks at a river together with its former bed and various hypothetical courses which it might have followed if there had been a different tilt to the plateau or a different volume of water. And while he in his mind is looking at a new river, the socialist in him is hearing new kindsof talk from the laborers who work by it. And, similarly, in the theatre, our spectator should find that the incidents set among such laborers are also accompanied by echoes and by traces of sketching.37

Brecht's art is not about Truth, but about the fitful pursuit of ambiguity. Ambiguity discomfits. It creates a vacuum in the place where there used to be easy answers. Fragmentation, likewise, convinces people that their truths are all provisional. It forces them to supply the missing pieces of a puzzle. Multiplicity insures that there will be something to puzzle over; that the natural, the obvious, and the convenient will be haunted by their opposites.

Benjamin and Brecht understood that the commercial exploitation of what were, at the date of their writing, the new instruments of publication would impress people with technical wizardry, replacing effect for substance, apolitical hedonism for political commitment. Brecht's insistence that an art that entertains but fails to instruct ultimately

---

[37]Ibid., p. 195.

leaves its recipients empty-handed was an acknowledgment of that danger. (It also tied together the fate of mass culture and mass education.) His critique of wanton emotionalism was a warning. Today, popular art that attempts to be critical of mainstream culture often affects a lack of affect, or, alternately, an unrealistically exaggerated amount of emotion. Both ploys are in the Brechtian tradition. The opportunities for functional transformation may have become more elaborate since Brecht's writing, but they have not essentially changed.

That is why Brecht's art should be understood as an alternate plan for the implementation of the technology of mechanical reproduction at its headwater. It advanced a kind of art that would use the technology to upset ideas from their cradle of existing power relations. Some of his innovations were absorbed into non-Brechtian forms of popular culture. Others were forgotten. Yet his defense of the potential behind technological art was as positive as Adorno's was denigrating. Thus, even though controversy exists over the ultimate nature and status of Brecht's contribution to twentieth-century radical culture (Adorno, for example, claiming him to be a Soviet apologist whose bad politics "stain" his aesthetics), the whole issue of commitment can be sidestepped by admitting the following.[38] Teaching audiences that a better use of the technology existed than what was

---

[38]Adorno, "Commitment," p. 186.

allowed into mass circulation fulfilled part of the agenda outlined by Benjamin in "The Author as Producer."

In the next chapter, the other side of the story will be heard. Adorno's position was that popular culture was inherently destructive to personal and political freedoms. He analyzed how technological art dimmed perception rather than sharpened it.

Chapter III

AUTONOMOUS CULTURE:
SURVIVING MESSAGE OF THE SHIPWRECKED

The Philosophy of Modern Music is the most empirical of Theodor Adorno's writings on aesthetic theory. It was published in 1948, in German, from earlier scattered articles and unpublished manuscripts written in exile in the United States. Its rather esoteric philosophical/sociological interpretation of the even more rarefied tradition of advanced music is the subject of this chapter for several reasons. For one, the author called the work an "appendix" to the core theoretical work he co-authored with Max Horkheimer, Dialectic of Enlightenment.[1] He intended it as an application to culture of the philosophy the two men developed in the 1940s. The Dialectic of Enlightenment approaches Western history as the two process of man's domination over nature and his mythification of this one-sided, violent relation.[2] Hence, the Philosophy of Modern Music shows how historical processes can be induced from aesthetic categories and, conversely, how aesthetic categories can be abstracted from

---

[1] Max Horkheimer and Theodor Adorno, Dialectic of Enlightenment (New York: Seabury, 1972).

[2] Jay, The Dialectical Imagination, Chapter 8.

historical processes. It thus illustrates one of the key notions of this writing, namely, that culture must be related to politics through structure rather than content.

Reason number two: by proceeding by "extremes" (Schoenberg, Stravinsky), Adorno hoped to illustrate the best and worst of what music could achieve under advanced capitalist conditions. Adorno did not believe that modern music had reached its present state of polarization as a matter of chance. Mass culture, which is mentioned directly only now and then, often in footnotes, causes high art to either drift toward commercialism or react fiercely against it. Independent or autonomous art, here exemplified by Schoenberg, is art which remains faithful to its inner demands despite the pressures of the market. Pseudo-autonomous art (Stravinsky) is art which appears to take a progressive form, but really panders to weak-minded publics out of mercenary considerations. Autonomous art loses its potential audience to mass culture, and thus has it to blame for its isolation. Dependent art is full of shams which prefigure the manipulative techniques of mass culture as well as encourage the spread of commercialism. Authentic high art aims to differentiate itself from mass art as well as raise people's consciousness about its shortcomings. Inauthentic high art is more perverse in its manipulation of people than the worst commercial art, because it is better at it. Autonomous and dependent art share a constellation of influences with mass culture. For this reason, Adorno's disquisitions on the music of Arnold Schoenberg and Igor Stravinsky in the Philosophy will be explored in depth.

The third reason is simply that Adorno's method is more elegant, restrained and reasoned when he deals with high culture, even of the specious kind, than when he is forced to grapple with the American popular culture he so despised. Since we are here concerned with mapping the relationship between aesthetic form and political ideology within mass culture, we stand to gain more from examining the patient structural analyses of the former, than the bilious denunciations of the latter. It is entirely possible that insights culled from Adorno's discussion of high art can be applied to popular art in ways unforeseen by Adorno himself.

Fourthly, Adorno was at a 180 degree angle from Benjamin and Brecht on the issue of popular culture. He was intolerant of it. Benjamin and Brecht thought it had social potential. Yet, despite their differences, all were agreed that aesthetic form, rather than content, was the source of art's political significance. It will not be until the later chapters of this dissertation that the structuralist definition of political ideology as a system of forms, rather than ideas, will be elaborated. Nonetheless, an assumption to this effect is already present in this earlier generation of aesthetic theory we are looking at now. In this literature, art is believed capable of puncturing presumptions by making people aware of their underlying structures. It is conceived of as an arena of competing formal practices where the public is taken out of its usual way of seeing the world and brought to new realizations. On this point, there is no argument. Dissension arises only when the three men describe which existing art accomplishes this perceptual rejuvenation, why and how. This chapter pins down Adorno's areas of agreement and disagreement with his theoretical adversaries.

By studying which kinds of art Adorno believed kept alive a challenge to the capitalist system and which helped sustain it, several things promise to be accomplished. Our understanding of the way aesthetic form's relationship to political ideology was historically conceptualized will grow. Further, we will be able to locate the source of the conflicting conclusions of our three theorists, and thus be better able to evaluate their pros and cons of mass culture. Having done that, we will be able to speak with more precision about why aesthetic form affects political consciousness, and what general characteristics it must possess in order to perform this function. Lastly, using Adorno as a foil for Benjamin and Brecht will highlight aspects of all three which do not show up in direct analysis.

Adorno wrote a seminal essay in 1938, prior to writing the <u>Philosophy</u>, which deserves mention before opening the discussion of his major treatise. The name of the essay is "On the Fetish Character of Music and the Regression of Hearing."[3] Adorno considered it a refutation of Benjamin's "Work of Art" essay.[4] In it, he discusses the commodification of music and its effects on individual and collective listening conduct. Commodification, he argues, obscures the substance of the work, its use value. Use value is what affords pleasure to the art lover. Exchange value is what makes him buy it. "Regressive listening" is listening that focuses on the second, the selling points, and not the subtle interplays which bring enjoyment.

The fetishism of music and the reification of perception such listening produces reconcile the consumer to the monopoly world of capitalism which immures him. By taming dissonance; by assimilating sounds of distance and depth (e.g. the pseudo-archaic sitar rock and roll of a motion picture like Gandhi); by rigging up "tricks" of individuation in minutely planned works of art (the musical conductor); and by fostering deconcentrated listening on a mass scale, irrational music binds the individual ever more firmly to a whole which controls and exceeds him. (We saw earlier that Max Horkheimer credits mass culture with this same ligative role.) "Masochism in listening" is a counterfeit pleasure that audiences fake, because they feel that by

---

[3] T. D. Adorno, "The Fetish Character of Music and the Regression of Hearing," in The Essential Frankfurt School Reader, ed. Andrew Arato and Eike Gebhart (New York: Urizen Books, 1978), pp. 270-300.

[4] Adorno, "Adorno to Benjamin," pp. 125-26.

identifying with the powers that control their lives, they will master them. Corrupt listening instills in the audience a false sense of ascendancy over the wayward social forces that make their lives so precarious. In return for the safety of its delusions, the modern audience forfeits the profound pleasure of inwardly motivated aesthetic contemplation. It is this pleasure which inspires people to struggle free from oppression. Its cheapening in mass culture breaks people's will to happiness and social change.

Adorno's Schoenberg essay followed this publication in time and logic. It attacks the same problem from the other end, that is, from the perspective of an art that is both 'in and for itself' and a counter-reaction to the culture industry. Adorno wants to promote recognition of ". . . the objective antinomies in which art, truly remaining faithful to its own demands, without regard for effect, is unavoidably caught up in the midst of heteronomous reality."[5] Art is exemplary of modern forms and degrees of domination because, until recently, it has always been treated as if it were above the harsh necessities of existence. That it, too, has now become mercantilistic betrays how deeply capitalism reaches into social life. For Adorno, the commercialization of art leads to an all-or-nothing situation. Art must either fend off the influence of the marketplace, or succumb.

---

[5] Adorno, <u>Philosophy of Modern Music</u>, p. xi.

Perhaps Adorno's key difference with Brecht lies in this very attitude. Brecht learned from film and radio in order to overturn them from within. His techniques were designed to "hit and run" mainstream art. Quite the contrary, Adorno brooked no communication with lower forms. In his view, the forces of subjugation innervate our institutions to their tips, leaving autonomous art no choice but to survive in exile from them. Adorno wrote in a 1960s essay on Brecht and political commitment in art that politics "migrate" to paragons of art, which offer solace from the degrading compromises of everyday life.[6] Adorno's search for an art of defiant perfection begins here in the discourse on Schoenberg. It explains, perhaps more than any other single point, his alienation from Benjamin and Brecht. The latter accepted popular art as having good and bad qualities. Adorno was made defensively utopian by circumstances.

Adorno begins his discussion of Schoenberg's music by analyzing the role of the art critic. He sees this role to be one of articulating the political implications of advanced music. Nonetheless, the critic finds himself in a quandary, due to the inaccessibility of the music he is charged with explaining. Radical music is opposed to ". . . the commercial depravity of the traditional idiom."[7] Publics mistake its lack of conformity for a failure of

---

[6] Adorno, "Commitment," pp. 177-95.

[7] Adorno, Philosophy of Modern Music, p. 5.

vision. They have "false musical consciousness." Since advanced music is experimental, there is no recourse to fixed, objective standards of right and wrong. Often, the composer is the only person qualified to justify his compositional choices, but is without the philosophic literacy necessary to do so. Enter the critic. The critic's job is to act as a mouthpiece for the artist, rationalizing in aesthetic and political terms the misunderstood or ignored music. (In other words, Adorno does not require the artist to jump the disciplinary walls that render him <u>incommunicado</u>, the way Benjamin does.) Yet, he has trouble performing his priestly function. His very mode of criticism is met with the same uncomprehending hostility as the ostracized music he is decoding meets with. His criticism is to commercial commentary what autonomous art is to dependent art.[8]

In sum, the two of them, the avant-garde and the critic of the avant-garde, are stowaways on the same breakaway iceberg called autonomous culture, shouting their insights (aesthetic, political) against the wind. The final irony is that the dulling of perception that occurs all over with the massification of culture--even the classics are debauched into snappy phrases and signature tunes--this coarsening of sensibility prevents advanced music from being heard by the society whose ills its horrifying dissonances mean to mirror. The critic's job is to make socio-economic

---

[8]Ibid., pp. 7-11.

and political imperatives the criteria for judging why a composition has taken the final shape it has. Without them, art can more easily be censored.

Explicitly stated in Adorno's argument that cultural truth goes innominate in the era of mass culture is the postulate that objective criteria of 'good' and 'bad' music do exist and abide through the vicissitudes of taste. Adorno holds that the perception of "logical consequence" or formal necessity in the plan of a composition is a better criterion than the mere passive enjoyment of "sensual sound."[9] He is thus at one with Brecht in making intellectuality preside over emotion in art, although what seems to be called for in Adorno's book is an almost mathematical approach to listening. Adorno objected to the fact that when electronic music came into existence, people stopped listening with their minds and gave themselves up to it bodily. He prefers a more sublimated, Platonic reception to art, unlike Benjamin, who based his positive opinion of film and photography on their sensuous realism. As Martin Jay points out in his famous study, the Frankfurt School, in contrast to more orthodox Marxists, accentuated the revolutionary importance of libido in cultural experience.[10] Here we see Adorno responding to what he perceives to be a challenge from another direction--the shallow hedonism of mass culture. The sexual

---

[9]Ibid., p. 12.

[10]Jay, The Dialectical Imagination, pp. 174-77.

emancipation of art must be entrusted to the stewardship of cognition. Uncontrolled pleasure will not be considered to fulfill the same revolutionary function as mentally mediated pleasure.

If protecting standards in art preserves the possibility of deep pleasure, then the critic will have a significant political contribution to make. His job will be both to expose the inferiority of the music put out by the culture industry, and oppose the apologists who legitimize it. Artistic commentary can never be divorced from political understanding. The exegesis of an opportunistic work cannot avoid talking about the context that makes it opportunistic. In order to point out a work's flaws, a critique should enlarge its scope to include the system that ordains them. Bad works of art are never just ill-conceived; they are duplicitous. Aesthetic criticism should also be political revelation.

Modern art squirms amidst multiple dilemmas. It is not absorbed by the society, because it sharpens awareness of what the society chooses not to face. In order to perform its naysaying function, it has to remain impervious to the economic demands eroding commercial culture. As a result of its purism, it loses access to the sphere of commodity circulation. People begin to find its language burdensomely foreign, since they never encounter it in commercial culture, and the languages they do meet do not require that they listen apprehensively. Modern art rejects the vernacular to speak the truth, in an idiom that people do not understand because it is not the vernacular. Its isolation is the outcome of growth: "The further this creative spirit advances towards autonomy, the more it alienates itself from a concrete relationship to everything dominated by it--human beings as well as materials."[11] (Is not this unavoidable irrelation what Lukacs mistook for and condemned as asociality?) Modern art is sundered from the world when it denies commerce and weakened if it accepts it. The modern artist, from his social quarantine, is even deprived of the resistance that has historically fed the creative drive. He has no intercourse with society, not even a negative one, snipped off as he is from tradition, from "all internal communication with ideas." Experimental music reels in disorientation.

It is up to the critic to battle advanced art's isolation. The analysis of advanced art is privileged, because it tracks the presence of totalitarian influences down to their byways in individual consciousness. To repeat, advanced music debouches from the fetishism of commercial culture. That which it thwarts, the determination of art's "right to existence" on the basis of its utility as an article of consumption, is precisely what denies it public standing in the first place. Because of its refusal to compromise, modern art is debarred from the main mechanism of

---

[11] Adorno, *Philosophy of Modern Music*, p. 20.

communication in capitalist society--the system of exchange value, the market. (Without publicity, who will witness its truth?) Our--the general public's--capacity to envisage alternatives wastes away as a result. We cannot take a broad view of the system with the aesthetic vocabulary the system traffics in, and we are insulated from the kind of art which can supply us with a fresh outlook. Without modern art, our projections of what a different society would look like extend a pitifully short ways. "In our totally organized bourgeois society, which has forcibly been made over into a totality, the spiritual potential of another society could lie only in that which bears no resemblance to the prevailing society."[12]

Adorno studied this problem at length in the Negative Dialectics.[13] We have lost the power to envisage not being ourselves. The institutions of domination stifle whatever differentiates itself over and against them in order to explain them and furnish an independent platform for acting in the world. Advanced music endures, as we shall see, from behind the defense of an extreme negativity. It is the great refusal, valuable for its lack of function or collaboration in capitalist society rather than for any positive purpose. In its extraneousness lies the font of those spiritual values the society will one day need to call upon if it is ever to transform itself. In the meantime, Adorno understakes his

---

[12]Ibid., p. 25.

[13]T. D. Adorno, Negative Dialectics (New York: Seabury Press, 1972).

exoneration of Schoenberg's music as a tragic geature of protest against the ignorance that makes it necessary.

Adorno's technical analysis of Schoenberg takes off from these introductory statements. According to him, Schoenberg's "revolutionary moment" comes when he expresses the negative emotions of the unconscious in his music directly, in the raw, rather than through standard imagery.[14] Normal conventions portrayed the violence of the psyche second-hand. Schoenberg's music strips away the figures usually surrounding it and irradiates it directly. It thumps out the rhythms of primal emotion the way an electrocardiogram translates heartbeats into a graphic picture. For example, hysteria is conveyed through a convulsion of sounds; anxiety, through a static, repetitive drumming. The music fluctuates back and forth between these two states with a relentless obsessionalism. The shibboleths of traditional music--harmonic flow, thematic development, melodic continuity--are discarded for the back and forth pendulum of a classic textbook nervous condition. The difference, then, between those who came before Schoenberg and Schoenberg is comparable to that between writing about anguish as content, in sober style, versus communicating it as the level of language itself, for example, by portraying seizures through a discombobulation of syntax.

The music's precise expression of the impulses of

---

[14]Adorno, *Philosophy of Modern Music*, pp. 30-31.

the unconscious reminds one of what Benjamin claimed the camera did for fluid behavior--parse it into its least components. In the age of Freud and technology, behavior has lost its metaphysical mystery. Schoenberg's composition reflects increases in scientific knowledge. But portraying the unconscious accurately called for new musical axioms. If Schoenberg had remained bound by the progressive structure of the symphony format, for example, he could not have represented cyclical psychological patterns. Yet, too, his innovations were important for more than their clinical correctness. They were revolutionary, because they voiced impulses that were dangerous to the rest of society. Schoenberg's "revolutionary moment" came when he invented a new language to articulate what past idioms muffled. His new language forced a re-evaluation of the values of the old one by bringing out its limitations. The ideal bourgeois world of truth and beauty, for instance, could not be viewed the same after art had become violently primitive (and primitively violent) through its own basic material.

The central importance of any piece of art is the relationship it sets up between subject and object, or individuals and material. Benjamin, you will recall, accepts the dissolution of the individual in the mass audience and the art that facilitates it. Adorno maintains that the relationship of the individual to art is more complicated than Benjamin allows, and, as a result, his cultural analyses suffer from an absence of dialectical development.[15] Art must reconcile the Self and nature, just as the human producer, through labor, appropriates the world about him and transcends his limited individuality, in turn. Art can make the mistake of overestimating the importance of the individual point of view (German Expressionism), or disregarding it by concentrating on physical building matter (The New Matter-of-Factness Movement). Schoenberg succeeded in striking a balance between the extremes of narcissism and reification where his contemporaries failed. Adorno sets out to explain how he did this, as well as why it was socio-politically significant, particularly considering the directions mass culture was taking at the time.

In the past, Adorno advises, the unification of subject and object was brought about by tonal variation. Style and balance were important techniques of integration. The first was the type of thematic progression that propelled the work forward; the second, the return of key phrases throughout the evolution of the theme. Schoenberg mastered the structural oppositions between the 'emotional' melody and the 'objective' bass, without using these balance and tension techniques. He intervenes directly in the organization of the scale, which makes melody and its complement possible in the first place.

Schoenberg's radicalism (again, radicalism has

---

[15]Adorno, "Adorno to Benjamin," pp. 110-20.

to do with rebuilding the architecture of an art form so that new aspects of reality may be fathomed) is starkest in the case of polyphony. Polyphony, also known as dissonance, had had a "prehistory" in the margins of Beethoven, Brahms and Wagner. Schoenberg's revolution of the rules of harmony instituted dissonance on a regular basis. After him, it was no longer an anomaly, to be called upon now and again as a bridge to further unison. A-tonality (another term for Schoenberg's system) ". . . asserts the principle of polyphony no longer simply as a heteronomous principle of emancipated harmony, which for the moment awaits reconciliation with harmony. He reveals it as the essence of harmony itself."[16] In the classical tradition, the single chord (three notes blended into one super sound) stood in opposition to the unblended sound or polyphony as the symbol of subjectivity. Schoenberg's scheme pushes this subjectivity to its limit by combining the triad in such a way as to prevent the three tones from coalescing. His system altered the method of selection of harmonics, by which certain tones were determined to "go with" other tones. It made it impossible for the three tones to fuse together. The accord of harmony was supplanted by a jointed, three-part unity. Dissonance (polyphony) became a matter of course.

The superiority of dissonance is that it enables us to construe harmony as we cannot by listening to harmony

---

[16] Adorno, *Philosophy of Modern Music*, p. 58.

itself. Dissonance ". . . articulates with great clarity the relationship of the sounds occurring within it--no matter how complex--instead of achieving a dubious unity through the destruction of those partial moments present in dissonance through 'homogeneous sound'."[17] From the point of view of a system based on consonance, dissonance can only be heard as deviation, as nonsense. From the opposite direction, however, dissonance elucidates harmony. It is a more exact statement of its consistency. Harmony becomes less awesome when the listener is given the recipe to it. Before Schoenberg, dissonance was just a mar on a smooth surface. After Schoenberg, it was a key to understanding.

What is the social significance of dividing the harmonic chord like this? Adorno likens the audible tone to the Self maintaining its unique identity amidst complex social associations. The individual is affirmed by Schoenberg's system in two ways. <u>Symbolically</u>, the music functions as a metaphor for the human One and the Many in optimal balance. Just as the individual note is redeemed, so is the individual viewpoint. Neither is forced into agreement with the whole, yet neither exists in isolation. <u>Practically</u>, the system helps the individual assume his rightful place in culture. In the harshness of the sound of dissonance, the individual verifies his own battle of existence. His private impressions are strengthened by being generalized thus

---

[17]Ibid., p. 59.

and so. Culture provides the objective correlate to his experience. Conversely, just as harmony subsumes the member tone, it sweetens the conflict of the individual member of society.

We have considered three inter-related factors so far in Schoenberg's music: the restructuring of the musical language; the sudden ability to express untoward realities with the new musical means; and a firming up of the individual in his relationship to culture as a result of the decrease in censorship. All three factors continue to inform Adorno's approach to twelve-tone composition. The latter is the culmination of Schoenberg's musical achievement. In the discussion of it that follows, Adorno emphasizes how artistic innovations improved the individual's relationship to culture and society.

First, it should be understood that twelve-tone compositions are built up out of the basic row. The rule of composition states that every note in the scale must be used once before it can be used again. This (completely arbitrary) rule applies to the single phrase as well as to the complex movement. In the old system, tones were selected at intervals of varying lengths. Their combinations could be manipulated. Each possessed a different character, depending on the distance between the notes and the way they were brought together. In Schoenberg's system, no such combinations are permitted. There are only consecutive series of atomized, disjunct notes. The order of the pitches is predetermined. Chords join notes in succession. In essence, the composer's choices are limited in advance to changing the row around through various sorts of inversion. He cannot wangle whatever new combinations he pleases--he is bound to a system that precludes excess initiative. This fact makes possible the reconciliation between subject and object, which Adorno sees as the political function of art.

Classical music overcame time, simple duration, by complicating and perfecting it with its own modalities of development. The progression of notes through a composition was, metaphorically, man moving through history, defining his temporality. (Music is ordered time, and thus quintessentially historical, opposed to the natural.) The twelve-tone technique replaced the continuous flow and elaboration of time within the classical composition with an incremental movement consisting of paraphrases and permutations of the row. The analyticalness of the technique--each musical moment is designated a place under an "omnipresent construction"--resolves the earlier flux into separate points. Each note obtains a schematic importance and independence from the rest. Thus, Adorno concludes, twelve-tone music negated time rather than enhanced it. The discontinuity between and the isolation of tones inhibited the sweep of sound. The musician no longer worked in "ideas" (the handling of a particular transition, the shade of a resonance, the shape of a melody), but rather exploited structure for its own sake. His efforts were so many ways of working out a beginning formula.[18]

Adorno claims that by dint of these constraints, the technique represents human society's conquest over nature.[19] The fabrication of the work has become so abstract, so spartan, its achievement no longer lay in illusion, but in correctness. How can the composer animate this thoroughly regimented repertoire? The preordinances of the system (every note disposed in advance) are what make the results so satisfying, while at the same time preventing them from being empty shows of skill. "The question which twelve-tone music asks of the composer is not how musical meaning is to be organized, but, rather, how organization is to become meaningful."[20] The subject (the composer) defers to a law of his own making and is set free from ego. He sublimates his instincts (nature) and, in return for his sacrifice, achieves new heights of creativity, freedom and individuality.

Since this assertion of the primacy of correctness over discretion gets to the heart of modernism's claim to be based on politics, I shall digress for a moment. It is generally agreed the modernism did not aspire to contest bourgeois values from the point of view of their content. Rather, it attacked those values by disaggregating their

---

[18] Ibid., pp. 60-63.

[19] Ibid., p. 64.

[20] Ibid., p. 67.

outer covering--language itself. The modernists bent the splendor of ideology through a spectrograph. Their boiling away of meaning into its physical byproducts caused great fragmentation. The part asserted itself against the whole, living on without it, usurping the larger plan which bestowed meaning upon it. For Schoenberg, it is the note at the expense of the motif. For poets or modernist writers generally, it is the word or even the Dadaist nonsense syllable at the cost of the sentence. Yet modernists denied they were making no sense at all. Just as dissonance allowed the listener to mark a well-defined multiplicity within the concord of a single chord (so what if it grated? It was true!), modernism believed it was getting people to reduce doxic ideas by consciously noticing their structure. After all, if we could be led to see the nuts and bolts in the finished spectacle; if the synthesis were to come undone; if every time we heard consonance, we referred knowingly to discordance, then these ideas would lose their power to narcotize us.

But there is also a political morality with Kantian overtones in Adorno's interpretation of modernism. "No rule proves itself more repressive than the self-determined one."[21] The composer invents and abides by a system of rules that disciplines him out of his willful, "coincidental," assumptions. His discipline likewise benefits the audience. It trains them. Twelve-tone music has an in-built capacity

---

[21] Ibid., p. 68.

to resist the easy answers and lazy listening propagated by mass culture. The severity of the technique fixes the audience's attention on it. The audience is constantly made aware of the plain notes and what the composer is doing to them. It becomes schooled in the method just by listening. It cannot be fooled by pyrotechnics or have its arbitrary prejudices catered to.

The price of making the scale into an object of contemplation is spontaneity. Where every detail is prearranged, there can be no unexpected turns, no sudden and thrilling contrasts (between high and low, for example). In the works of Schoenberg, ". . . all musical minutiae are predetermined by the totality, and there is no longer any interaction between the whole and the part. The commanding disposition of the totality banishes the spontaneity of the moment."[22] This ruling out of <u>play</u> is not as regrettable as it might seem, however, since in our alienated society, true improvisation is beyond anybody's reach. It we try to go our own way, we are bound to repeat in endless disguises our neurotic, truncated relation to the world. Adorno makes this clear in his writings on jazz.[23] He reduces its supposedly free style to a merry-go-round of a few, redundant phrases. His position is that jazz remains closed within its own

---

[22] Ibid., p. 71.

[23] T. D. Adorno, "Perennial Fashion--Jazz." in <u>Prisms</u>, trans. Samuel and Shierry Weber (London: Neville Spearman, Ltd., 1967), pp. 119-32.

undeveloped theory, doomed to repetition, even while imagining that it is taking the audience on a jaunt to the beyond. That audiences clamor for it anyway only goes to show how much they fear breaking away from familiar ground. (In fact, twelve-tone technique is so far the opposite of this pretentious spontaneity that by the time one arrives at the end of the row, which means all the other possibilities have been depleted, the final pitch has so much "terminal force," Schoenberg must "quote" from traditional forms like the refrain to overcome with rhythm its peremptory finish.) It is up to advanced music to combat the illusions of freedom and spur-of-the-moment rained upon us by commercial art. Twelve-tone construction is the antidote to commercial culture's false promises.

Adorno asserts that every facet of Schoenberg's music is reminiscent of the historical conditions that gave rise to it. Because dissonance is no longer at the discretion of the composer, but is inherent in the execution of the technique, it has become transpersonal. It is not a composer's voluntarily nihilistic gesture, but a repercussion of the system. "Dissonances arose as the expression of a tension, contradiction and pain. They took on fixed contours and became 'material'. They are no longer the media of subjective expression. . . . They become characters of objective protest."[24] In other words, twelve-tone technique

---

[24] Adorno, Philosophy of Modern Music, p. 86.

was invented at a time in history when pain and brutality could no longer be brushed aside. A system had to be created that shuddered with their presence. The logic of the system had to express them so as to make clear they were part of the outside world, not somebody's private torment. Twelve-tone composition did this by making every sound clash with the next, by normalizing conflict. Such a system is revolutionary because it gives people a new means to gauge the world.

Adorno stresses that even twelve tone composition's inadequacies are products of the times. Its failure with the large form, for example, is indicative of its critique of alienated society. The large form, e.g., the symphony, relieves all tensions within the work by its end. Modern music maintains that the situation of the world renders such finitude facile. It rejects what is rounded-off, logically continuous and at its full extent, either in form or content. In it, discontinuity and fragmentation are wielded as "critical weapons." They are used to protest the impossibility of realizing one's capacities, talents, visions and ambitions under capitalism. The amputation capitalist life subjects us to without our knowledge or consent consists of the belief that because this is what we are at the present moment, this is all we can be. Modern music denounces such loss of potential by refusing to bring the composition to completion. Its aggressive lack of finality becomes a cry of hope in this "age of the total planning of substructure." That is its reason for existing. Through the stridency of its example, it announces that art will not pursue ultimate development as long as everyday life does not afford the same opportunity.

The fragment is plainly a renunciation: "The triumph of subjectivity over heteronomous tradition--the freedom of allowing every musical moment to stand for itself without imputation--is achieved at a very high cost."[25] And yet it is also an escape from dutiful discourse, from the warp that finished designs inevitably introduce into art. Benjamin and Adorno overlap rather ironically on this point as well. Whereas Adorno wrote systematically in praise of the fragment, Benjamin wrote fragmentarily in defense of his choice not to be systematic.

The only mission left to purposefully function-less music is to depict "a picture of total repression but, by no means, the ideology thereof."[26] Naming ideology is not the same thing as broadcasting it. Mass-produced music does the latter. Its production techniques confirm its partnership with the status quo. Statistical streamlining (tailoring a song to a market, for instance) and division of labor (one person writes the lyrics, another the accompaniment, still another produces) betray that art has become quite

---

[25] Ibid., p. 104.

[26] Ibid., p. 113.

comfortable with commodity manufacture. By contrast, the "innocent endeavors" of the twelve-tone composers are old-fashioned. They do not manufacture music in accordance with market surveys. Imagination, skill and reverence for tradition inspire their unscientific creative activity. Yet their methods are all the more rational for avoiding those of "propagandistically constructed" music.[27] Commercial music eases a person's adjustment to life under capitalism (for example, by purveying the plodding rhythms that make mindless labor a little less hard to bear). It does not cultivate the listener's sensibilities any more than it does the creator's. Only pre-industrial (autonomous) music is not conceived with the maintenance needs of the capitalist system at heart.

There is, according to Adorno, a contradiction between the productive forces of technological culture and their conditions of production. Adorno's argument with Benjamin over mass culture here reaches its apogee. The technologically advanced product of mass culture represents a misuse of the instruments of production. No matter what difficulties the twelve-tone system comes up against (the isolation of the subject, his seeming loss of the right of expression, his inability to express this inability), its aporias are of a more intellective bent than those of, say, the film industry. The film industry uses angles and surfaces without broadening our understanding of its methods. It

---

[27]Ibid., p. 113.

fantasizes reality. Picasso's Cubist painting, which is auratic, teaches us more about the reflexes of photography than does photography in its present state of development. Cubism paints the solid object as existing on many planes at once. It takes a main feature of technologically-influenced perception--the ability to maintain several counter versions of a single object--what Benjamin called "test"-- and studies it in the abstract. Film could formally present its own formalizing influences. Instead, it disorients the viewer with hallucinatory antics.

Benjamin cared less that art clarify to the spectator the artifice behind the image. In "The Work of Art" essay, he implied that the role of avant-garde art was to prefigure technological changes in art, which, once instituted, would become part of the average person's vocabulary. Photography, unlike Cubism, could do what it was equipped to do (multiply perspectives, delineate detail, interrupt movement), without having to be blatant about it. What Adorno took for absolute fiat, the baring of the role of the equipment in the image, Benjamin regarded as a temporary measure. Many of Benjamin's arguments in favor of popular culture owe their validity, or lack thereof, to who was right.

A summary is in order. There are three kinds of art being discussed here: classical or traditional bourgeois art (Benjamin's term for it was "auratic"; Marcuse's "affirmative"; and Adorno's "hermetic" or sometimes "autonomous"); avant-garde art (advanced, modern, modernist, critical and radical are all synonymous terms), and mass art (post-auratic, commercial, dependent, technological). Classical art--the example I have been calling on is tonal music--embodied utopianic longings for beauty, freedom and enlightenment. It was 'autonomous' insofar as it strove for perfection within its own sphere, undaunted by economic scarcity or "the realm of needs." In the history of the bourgeoisie, the function of this type of art was to nourish hope that truth and beauty existed in the world.

Avant-garde art--Schoenberg's atonalism, fragmentism in general--was classical art's determinate negation. Arising in the early twentieth century, it ridiculed venerable aesthetic standards of beauty and propriety. Its ultimate aim was to challenge art's independence from everyday life. In defilement of finely wrought bourgeois art, it cultivated ugliness. In mockery of traditional rhetoric, it articulated itself in fragments and non-meaning. Its tactics were meant to show that bourgeois art, in all its ethereality and self-seriousness, was really just a middle-class plastic surgery of brute existence. Art which pretended to be above warring class interests was ideological. By attacking the form of such art, avant-gardism believed itself to be blasting its well-composed lie.

The third kind of art is the one being talked about

in Chapters I and II. It was typified by photography and cinema, although today any art which is realized through mechanical media falls into this category. Technological art spelled the end of an era for classical art by introducing mechanical procedures of production and reception into an area that had proved unknown to them in the past. These techniques depreciated the singularity and spiritual force of classical art--in Benjamin's terms--they spoiled its "aura." The machine (i.e. the camera) was now capable of registering reality more accurately and vividly than the do-it-by-hand artist. Objective manufacturing processes were taking over for personal vision. Mechanical art thus did through its revolution in the means of production what avant-garde art had attempted to do didactically and polemically through small, disruptive movements. Art, no longer held as sacred, was brought much closer to everyday life.

In fact, although avant-garde art itself was not mechanized--it had this in common with its traditional precursors--it did construct its objects to look mechanistic. It did this as a way of taking the luster of vaunted bourgeois values. The theory was that delineating the structure of an image the way the camera did dispelled illusion. Making prominent to the audience the scaffolding of a work of art was a way of deriding its pretensions. It was supposed to cause cynicism in people toward society's great symbols. Just as psychoanalysis gives a person control over his impulses by analyzing them, avant-gardism gives him a handle on ideology the same way. Science replaces mysticism. Schoenberg's portrayal of the unconscious is an example of avant-garde art's preference for the engineering behind feelings rather than their pathos. By contrast, mechanical reproduction, which was the model for radical art, passed itself off as natural and immediate, at least, according to Adorno. Says the critic of mass culture and its "replica realism," it is ". . . an advertisement for the world through its duplication."[28]

Adorno believes that both classical and avant-garde art mounted a protest against the state of society, the first, by providing a standard against which present reality could be judged and found wanting; the second, by puncturing high art's self-containment. In addition, radical art preserved the critical thrust of traditional art in the very manner in which it mutilated it. Its rebellion was intentional, scrupulous, aware of what it was rebelling against, and thus resonating with it through an inverse symmetry. We saw, for instance, how polyphony, although seeming to scrap harmony altogether, actually exposed its welding.

It was this tether to the past which mass culture did not have. Against Benjamin, Adorno ventured the proposition that mass art was not post-auratic at all. Benjamin's theory

---

[28] T. D. Adorno, "Culture, Criticism and Society," in Prisms, p. 34.

about mechanical reproduction's demystification of high art was well and good, but the fact remained that mass culture never worked through the contradictions of traditional art (its glorification of its subject matter versus its indifference to actual living conditions). Avant-garde art's relationship to the past was that of a dialogue. Mass art's relationship to the past--a rupture. Commercial art never became cognitive and disenchanting through a confrontation with the old (the example of photography above). It never cited the past in its indiscretions. It just took over by force. Notice that Adorno sees the "catharsis" talked about by Benjamin--the throwing into disarray of traditional art --as a sinister strategy rather than an accidental dislocation caused by the machinery: "The hermetic work of art belongs to the bourgeois, the mechanical work to fascism, and the fragmentary work . . . to utopia."[29] Adorno will also not admit that within mass culture, countervailing symbolic practices exist, as per Brecht and film.

Now that the lines have been drawn, it becomes easier to understand Adorno's intolerance for mass culture. The issue of contiguity with the past is probably primary in explaining it. Innovation that does not simultaneously rescue the past from itself leads to a breakdown of individuality, the likes of which Adorno demonstrated in The

---

[29] Adorno, Philosophy of Modern Music, p. 126.

Authoritarian Personality.[30] The effort and skill required to understand a great work of art is a "social demand." It is comparable to reading, where one must master a set of skills to share a rapport with a community of language users, living and dead. Seen in this light, twelve-tone music's terrific complexity (it was often accused by critics of being overly demanding) functions as "an instrument of freedom."[31] Its arduousness is a means of enforcing standards in an age when no exertion and, therefore, no sociality or communality are asked of the cultural recipient. Twelve-tone-ism saves the musical experience from the historical atrophy of certain possibilities of hearing. It sustains certain strenuous skills of audition. Indeed, Adorno's decision to publish earlier drafts of portions of this work in German, even though residing in the United States, reflects the diasporic mentality underlying his interpretation of twelve-tone music as the remnant of a devastated, scientific culture.[32]

Remember, too, that the significance of the loss of authentic musical experience ("The possibility of music itself has become uncertain.") would not be of secondary significance to a theorist like Adorno.[33] The Frankfurt

---

[30] Adorno, The Authoritarian Personality (New York: W.W. Norton & Co., 1950).

[31] Adorno, Philosophy of Modern Music, p. 124.

[32] Jay, The Dialectical Imagination, Chapter 6.

[33] Ibid., p. 112.

School saw culture as a realm of freedom. Its preview of non-alienated society was necessary to give people a reason to resist domination, not to mention the power and vision to do so. It was for its sake ("the promise of happiness") that revolution demanded to be waged, far more than for the utilitarian economic reasons advanced by more orthodox Marxists. As utopianism was for Marx, autonomous culture was for Adorno, the medium of man's aspirations toward emancipation. If it were rooted out, then the inkling it gave men of a better world would dissipate too.

Moreover, in Dialectic of Enlightenment, Adorno and Horkheimer theorized that advanced capitalism, the apparatus of economic production and that of psycho-social domination have come to overlap. (Hence, their interest in the "soft sell" authoritarianism of American popular culture.) In contrast to traditional Marxist theory, they no longer believed art to be part of the superstructure or a way of shoring up more fundamental power relations through ideas. They maintained that works of art either directly fed into the relations of production (mass culture) or exhibited them in their true light (autonomous culture). Autonomous works (in the avant-garde meaning of the term) ". . . are concealed social essence quoted as phenomenon."[34] That is, they appear to be one person's subjective interpretation of reality, but are actually concretions of its fundamental

---

[34] Ibid., p. 131.

meaninglessness. Art has survived into a ghastly world in order to document it by denying the possibility of art. "Modern music sees absolute oblivion as its goal. It is the surviving message of despair from the shipwrecked."[35]

The only uncompromising role left to art in the world after Auschwitz is to take a stand against all positive meaning. (Such meaning is always tainted. The most one can do is interfere with the forms that keep it afloat. One can report on the lie, but not debate with it.) Advanced music is a highly structured, meaning-resistant nullity. It undermines the high-mindedness of traditional music in the ways discussed above: through fragmentism, steadfast attention to structure (the notes remain unsculpted, in their original state), and systemic integration (the total although absolutely meaningless legality of the order of the twelve pitches). If bourgeois art celebrated the order of things, avant-garde puts a crimp in the celebration. By remaining impervious to capitalist ways of thinking and perceiving, it serves as a measure of our social homogenization. In its profound negativity, it contradicts, not this or that belief, but the entire way in which we organize meaning.

Modern music is the apotheosis of negativity, the negativity belonging to the world. The composition proclaims, with its own formal necessity, the downfall of meaning. Adorno ends his discussion of Schoenberg on this theme.

---

[35]Ibid., p. 133.

Later on, however, he will back off slightly from the belief finally expressed in these pages that advanced music is despair incarnate. Even Schoenberg's "Survivors of Warsaw," he says, repugnant and unequivocal though it may be, "embarrasses" by using the victims' pain to create a work of art, to bring pleasure.[36] All art is a transmutation, a description, rather than, as said before, a "congealed social essence." It thus will always have something of the ideological about it. Adorno cannot entirely escape the contradictions of his absolutism.

Stravinsky

Modern art is the utmost in denial. And, yet, it, too, has the ersatzes, of which Adorno is here concerned with the music of Igor Stravinsky. Where the form goes astray, where it does not possess this compelling, not-of-this-world rationality (Schoenberg's music is critical insofar as it is non-native to our ways of thinking), there will be an instance of cultural domination. Adorno decodes the meanings of art's internal errors in such a way that the social and the formal spell each other out.

The reader should pay particular attention in this upcoming section to why Adorno considers Stravinsky's music (and by implication mass culture) so ignominious. That is to say, Stravinsky's work is treated as particularly

---

[36] Adorno, "Commitment," pp. 188-89.

insidious for the following reasons. It bears some of the emblems of an advanced consciousness. Regrettably, it serves as a model for many cultural radicals. Lastly, it calls itself 'avant-garde'. There is thus a special urgency in the way Adorno exposes where and how this music falls short of his standards of autonomy. In part, Adorno's critique of Stravinsky will be a denunciation of many of the most important trends to come out of the avant-garde in the last half of the century. Arguing against many of the conventions of non-conventional art, he uses Stravinsky as an object lesson to show how dehumanizing, commercial forces have made headway into the last strongholds of authentic culture.

Adorno has previously argued that radical culture uses structure and expression to buttress the individual and bring him under an overarching culture. Stravinsky's music, on the contrary, is "a turning point against the subject."[37] It weakens the individual.

One of the ways Stravinsky's music enervates the individual is by glorifying folk music. The studied simplicity of his orchestral works provides a comparable experience to that of a fairgrounds observer or an intellectual attending a popular concert. It symbolizes light entertainment as an alternative to developed listening, the distraction of the "music hall, vaudeville and circus," as a

---

[37]Adorno, *Philosophy of Modern Music*, p. 143.

substitute for the practiced consumption of the connoisseur.[38] Much of vanguard art has followed the royal road of regression, so Adorno's critique of it in Stravinsky will have wider implications. One of them is the importance of aesthetic "infantilism," or what may be called the defense of inarticulateness, as a response to ideological "fast-talk." The other is the role of the intellectual in legitimizing mass culture.

But for now, it is the individual who is at issue. The paramount importance Stravinsky's music gives "the mechanical factor" portends the demise of the political, cultural, and ethical subject. Mechanization (the wind instruments being made to sound like a street vendor's organ; the "soulful strings," the hallmark of the great individualist works, being "perverted into a joke") quenches the human spark in classical music. The violence and wierdness of mechanical sonorities incite audiences to irrational behavior. They dehumanize sound.

Like the Surrealist fascination with African sculpture, Stravinsky too is enamored of the idea of the primitive and the role of instinct in art. His ballet "Rites of Spring" is about an aboriginal tribe's ritual murder of a young girl who it has made the scapegoat of its problems. Ostensibly, the use of myth in this ballet is to jolt people out of the dullness they have lapsed into through constant exposure to

---

[38] Ibid., p. 145.

liberal ideology.[39] In reality, it seduces audiences with the thrill and shock of the macabre. In other words, Stravinsky turns to myth to mask the decline in musical sensitivity described in the preceding paragraph. He appeals to audiences' base instincts on the theory of its being an anti-bourgeois thing to do.

The theme of regression is a mainstay of Adorno's analysis of both Stravinsky and mass culture. Stravinsky is the theorist and imagist of regression *par excellence* and even more interesting in this respect than his countless imitators. His composition is supposed to exorcise the fear of psycho-social reversion by externalizing it. It aims to conquer the fear of barbarism "magically," by playing it out theatrically in both the music and the narrative. Accordingly, the dance scenes in "Rites" are full of archaic-looking mimicry, rigid poses and robotified demeanor. The musical score is rude, "witty," cleverly bizarre and backward sounding. Adorno believes that the musical insult to Western civilization behind Stravinsky's outlandish crudeness couches "the liquidation of the subject."[40]

Part I has left us with the general idea that a work of art is anti-ideological, or at least has the potential of being so, when it fundamentally transforms the musical language. Adorno's key objection to Stravinsky's music is that it fails to make structural kinds of changes,

---

[39]Ibid., p. 147.

[40]Ibid., p. 148.

that it is tonally tame. In essence, it works its strangeness through a device called "polytonality," as defined by Adorno to mean the juxtapositioning of "interlaced sounds of varying and spatially separated musics, as at a fair."[41] Polytonality leaves the systemic relations of tonality untouched, in contrast to Schoenberg's music, which redefined them. Shock effects are produced by combining incompatible sounds into patterned complexes. The dissonance that results is montagic, in no way the outcome of a methodological overhaul. In contrast to twelve-tone dissonance, particular structures have no connection to the totality. They are grouped together randomly, without syntax. In sum, the "exhaustion" of technique so apparent in Stravinsky's music cannot be excused by the composer's pretense to avoid all pretense to sophistication.[42] The change from the past is more one of impoverishment than radical innovation.

Bear in mind that Adorno makes the awesomely intricate Schoenberg his measure of radical excellence. Brecht, however, used polytonality to create a cognitive counterpoint in the spectator. That is, if you start out with a scene of, say, an army going to battle, and the musical accompaniment, rather than a battle hymn, is circus music; then the latter "comments" on the scene by not comporting with it. The fact that it is ill-suited to the subject matter causes

---

[41]Ibid., pp. 151-52.

[42]Ibid., pp. 152-55.

a turnabout in the spectator. The spectator wonders, "Is the music accusing the army of clownishness? Is going to war the act of a buffoon?" Meaning is brought into question by causing it to sit between two stools. This particular kind of counterpoint is important, not for the quality of its music or its plot, but for the cognitive skip their junction causes in the spectator. Interestingly, Brecht believed that bawdy saloon music was more effective for making people hesitate over their assumptions than serious music. Adorno was utterly unable to sympathize with this way of thinking. To him, circus and vaudeville music were worthless except as apocrypha of pre-capitalist social formations.

But, returning to Stravinsky, Adorno emphasizes how the work's lack of planning disorients the listener. The shock effects of the music are unchannelled, unmotivated conceptually. They are not parried by a "resisting ego," or by a subject who, anticipating assault, arms himself against them with anxiety.[43] (The reference to Benjamin's distraction theory and what Adorno called its "shock-like seduction" is fairly plain.)[44] The crashes and bangs of the orchestra are never meant to be processed by the audience or sublimated into language, as they were for Schoenberg. The musical subject--man in industrial society--just absorbs them. He does not drive them back with his own defenses (awareness).

---

[43]Ibid., pp. 156-57.

[44]Adorno, "Adorno to Benjamin," p. 123.

He is physically harassed rather than mentally stimulated. The violence he is subjected to has little to do with the basic musical relationships. It interferes with his sense of judgment rather than hones it. Thus, although the music, by adopting myth, rejects unthinking conformity with bourgeois society, it really bludgeons the individual into a much more thoroughgoing submission. Attacking him at the level of the body rather than the head makes him culturally passive. The old bourgeoisie was never that.

Audiences accept the effrontery. They respond with sado-masochistic glee to the murder of the young girl in "Rites." They consent to the extirpation of the victim (and of their own egos) as a way of appeasing the horde. In other words, the audience identifies with the aggressor in order to allay its own fears of victimization. The connection between mass response and sado-masochism is a familiar one in Adorno's writings on mass culture. In a letter to Benjamin, Adorno disputes Benjamin's claim that audiences respond more critically as a group because they ignite each other's reactions. Their laughter at the pathos of Charlie Chaplin films is cruel rather than enlightened. (Chaplin pokes fun at everything from Nazism to unemployment. Adorno believes audiences' willingness to share in the fun is pathological.)[45] Adorno pictures Stravinsky's music the same way. It sets up the audience to sympathize with the

---

[45] Ibid., pp. 123-24.

group in the story, who turn against and lay waste the outsider. He sees it as a manifesto of mass culture, with its peculiar brand of totalitarianism. When Stravinsky flouts bourgeois norms, it is not liberating. It is going from the frying pan into the fire.

As the above paragraph makes clear, Adorno interprets Stravinsky with psychological categories that he never uses with Schoenberg. He sees in Stravinsky's musical regression a corresponding psycho-social regression on the part of the audience. The members of the audience gaze upon their nemesis (as symbolized by that of the slaughtered girl) with the boredom of schizophrenics. Adorno compares audience response to "Rites of Spring" with the way certain societies have been found to react to war--with mass catatonia, benumbing, stupefaction. Bourgeois society's acclaim of Stravinsky is proof of its decadence. The individual is running scared. If he stands by, while his independence gets demolished, it is because he hopes to avoid worse catastrophe. Culture under these circumstances can no longer be said to be a haven from the workaday world. It has become the altar atop which society sacrifices the right of its members to private identities. Culture ritually sacrifices the right of individuality as a means to mollify the impersonal forces that threaten its doom.[46]

---

[46] Adorno, Philosophy of Modern Music, p. 159.

The destruction of the self is necessitated by modern conditions, but it is played out in the guise of the primitive. That way, the audience does not have to deal with its real fears. Situating the event in a distant epoch codes the panic which inspires it. At the same time, the sound which conveys the story is baldly mechanical. The incorporation of bleak industrialized noise, e.g., the drone of a sewing machine, into music degrades it. It does not signify a physiological transformation of modern man's hearing, as Brecht claimed, but rather a total capitulation to mindless forces. It bespeaks the end of musical "humanism," the end of the infusion of the human spirit into the instrument. That Stravinsky could have elicited interest in these despised sounds testifies, not to the transformation of hearing, but to the vanquished state of expression, to the victory of alienation. The tumult his body music stirred up in the listener was bad enough. The introduction of workplace sounds into formal culture is more menacing still. The rationale behind it is that converting alienated experience into art redeems it. Raising ordinary noise to the level of intentionality serendipitously sanctifies it. Adorno rejects this explanation. To him, the drone of a sewing machine at a concert is a tragedy. It is the musician's ineffectual gesture of revolt against his own powerlessness. "The schizophrenic demeanor of Stravinsky's music is a ritual which attempts to overcome the coldness of the world."[47]

Music henceforth overwhelms. Its theoretical problematics are shunned. The interrelations between instruments, duration and structure, hereafter, interests neither composer, nor audience. The music is pumped for its effects, all of them, material, superficial, "almost athletic" in character.[48] The individual is not integrated into or by the listening experience. He listens dissociatedly, unable to emote to the stiff steps of the dancers or the spastic mannerisms of the music, but nonetheless reacting bodily to their disconcerting quality. His experience correlates with the disunity of the material, a disunity that comes as a result of Stravinsky's forced forgetfulness of the past. Ironically, Adorno's language recalls Benjamin. It would appear that many of the changes Benjamin endorsed as "exhibition value"--the surface appeal of the new art, its crass exploitation of thoroughbred tradition--are here interpreted as symptoms of a sick society. For Benjamin, the purely sensual was a garden of delights; for Adorno, it was a desert.

Adorno can draw such different conclusions from Benjamin because of the analogies he makes with psychological processes. In the Schoenberg reading, we are always inside the musical experience. We learn how its structures stand in relation to each other in comparison to how the structures

---

[47]Ibid., p. 170.

[48]Ibid., p. 173.

of social complexes stand vis a vis each other. What we are dealing with is a relationship of homology between separate sets of structures and their internal relations. From the outward contours of the two classes of phenomena, aesthetic and social, we can tell very little. It is only with structural investigation that matching patterns begin to emerge; the identity of the dissonating tone in the plural of the chord/ the identity of the social individual in the plural of the sodality. I mention this methodological point here to demonstrate that Adorno's commentary of Stravinsky is woven out of a different theoretical fiber.

With Stravinsky (as with Adorno's approach to jazz), psychological paradigms unite the social and the aesthetic. The social and the aesthetic resemble each other rather than have parallel structural proportions. The shift is subtle, but pivotal. Adorno tries to convince readers of the relation between Stravinsky's suppression of the subject and schizophrenia, not through immanent structural analysis, but through the imputation of qualitative reactions to the audience upon exposure to his music. Audiences are said to _identify_ with the collective lynchmob in "Rites." Why is it not possible that they simply notice and take pleasure in the music's deviance? Mechanicalness and rigidity in music and dance do not necessarily deserve to be equated with psychotic states in which mechanicalness and rigidity are in evidence. So much of Adorno's obloquy against popular music depends upon this shift from structures (i.e. electronic strings) to emotional processes (self-deception, subservience, fear), without his ever justifying it methodologically. His discussion of Stravinsky veers off into the descriptive; Benjamin's and Brecht's discussion of popular art confine themselves to formal parameters of perception. For example, Brecht's concern with pacing the text properly is not out of consideration for <u>what</u> audiences will think or feel, but rather that they will be given enough reaction time to do either at all.

A further example of Adorno's psychologizing is the following. Adorno compares the depersonalization of expression in Stravinsky to the psychotic state of "hebephrenia" or the impassiveness of the patient toward the world about him. He goes on to say that the frigidity and emotional vacancy of this condition is not due to the total loss of affect, so much as to the patient's inability to exude emotion. The patient is unable to invest himself libidinally in his outlying universe. Stravinsky's music, which severs subject and object, brings about a similar autism in the subject by depriving him of his power of expression. A person makes an impact on his surroundings by articulating speech. The muddle of Stravinsky's music leaves the typical listener mute and introverted. It denies the subject the tools to possess the world.[49]

---

[49] Ibid., p. 176.

Film, where "picture, word and sound are disparate," causes the same schism in the subject as Stravinsky's music.[50] A very large leap is made between the divisive procedures of mechanical reproduction and the divided consciousness of the onlookers, on the one hand, and disease on the other. Benjamin could be mobilized against him here by saying that the atomization of film is akin to atonality's unit-by-unit constructivism. In both, one starts with and compiles bare elements. In both, the elements remain in a mixture rather than a compound. Twelve-tone music and film might even be said to be homologous in the same sense in which the segmented tone represents the human socius. It is only Adorno's reliance on psychology which permits him to overlook their latent similarity. He is loathe to admit that film can pierce illusion by dismantling the image as successfully as advanced music.

The issue behind many of Stravinsky's pseudo-innovations has to do with art's relationship to the past. When Benjamin spoke of the "catharsis" of mechanical reproduction, he referred to the liberty it took with traditional forms. The illogical, dream-like juxtapositioning of words and images of the Surrealists was a politicization of this material freedom. (The Surrealists claimed it brought the liberating force of the unconscious into the drudgery of everyday life.) To Benjamin, these kinds of Surrealist

---

[50]Ibid., p. 176.

techniques, through their cultivation of incongruity, caused people to jettison old habits of perception. Stravinsky himself made use of them. He composed an oneiric music, piecing together bits of popular idioms--the polka, jazz--the way an actual dream assembles material out of recent waking contacts.

Adorno, on the other hand, is disturbed by this arbitrary neighboring of elements. The theory that the unconscious should determine syntax in art as it does in dreams sounded too tenuous to him to work. Worse, it produced an art that could not stand up to fascist philistinism. Hitler's academics were able to dismiss the avant-garde's neo-primitivism quite easily because it did not have roots in the past. More to the point, when such techniques were not actually dangerous, they were puerile. Stravinsky pretended to be above convention by incorporating commercial idioms like ragtime into his repertoire. In reality, his derring-do was only an adolescent rebellion against the fathers of European music, a disrespect typical of the authoritarian personality's attitude to authority. Socially, his experiments only served to dignify sordid sounds. Only Schoenberg's scrupulous sense of system protected against this kind of loose thinking.[51]

Adorno concludes on the issue of authenticity, the very one, as we shall see momentarily, that he began with.

---

[51] Ibid., pp. 181-84.

Authenticity consists of the commitment and know-how to create within time-honored constraints. Schoenberg renounced authenticity when he invented entirely new, <u>ad hoc</u> solutions to technical problems posed by his brave, new beginnings. Twelve-tone construction was the unpremeditated answer to dilemmas which sprung up in the course of composition. Its final shape could not have been anticipated. Hence, it is truly authentic to the degree it never intended to be so. Schoenberg was able to coin new, much-needed expressions for unrecorded problems because he put method before ostentatious innovation. Just as the individual finds himself by exploring uncharted waters, so art becomes revolutionary.

Stravinsky's "contrived style of objectivity," by contrast, inhibits the creation of new artistic languages.[52] It hangs over everybody's head an autocratic standard of authenticity. It waves banners at the audience. Commercial culture does the same by hammering away at the idea of originality in its marketing of cultural commodities. Audiences respond to the claim of authenticity, because it gives them something to hook into (the exchange value of the music). But there is a built-in repression to pre-defining what authenticity should look and sound like. It penalizes those individuals struggling in the dark toward new systems in the manner of Schoenberg. A pretense to originality such as Stravinsky's prevents the crystallization of the new

---

[52] Ibid., pp. 212-17.

forms that revivify consciousness. Warning audiences what to expect beforehand only teaches them to reject what is unfamiliar and truly experimental as failed variants of the prototype. Speaking of Stravinsky, Adorno concludes:

> The qualities of myth which fascinate him are its image of eternity, of salvation from death, and that which came into being in time through the fear of death and through barbaric suppression. The falsification of myth documents an elective affinity with authentic myth. Art would perhaps be authentic only when it had totally rid itself of the idea of authenticity, or the concept of being-so-and-not-otherwise.[53]

Before moving on, a couple of concluding points may help to clarify Adorno's relationship to Benjamin and Brecht. First, there is an assumption in all three of them that if people are given the opportunity to analyze correctly, they will see through the charades of the ruling class. Adorno lodged this power of perspicacity in a small cultural elite. Benjamin and Brecht enfranchised the masses with it.

There was a common understanding, too, about language and art. Through them, people were thought to rationalize the given or bristle against it. The same formal qualities of language and art were reputed to encourage them toward the latter: fragmentism, ambiguity, and multiplicity. Fragmentism prevented the parts of a composition from bleeding together into a smooth whole. Writers on radical aesthetics agree there is something about the way people live their lives under capitalism that makes this

---

[53]Ibid., p. 217.

lack of resolution, this in-built ambiguity, hard to bear. Benjamin believed mass culture brought the tension of ambiguity to a new pitch. Adorno wondered if mass culture costumers could hear anything but monotony.

It is difficult to say who was right and who was wrong in these debates. In all likelihood, they were all right <u>and</u> wrong. We have lived to see techniques of cognitive disorientation milked to capacity by advertising and cash-register culture. On the other hand, we have seen the Bertolt Brechts of this world come along and "hold the camera" on evidence that is incriminating to the social system. Both tendencies subsist in modern mass culture and perhaps, to that degree, Benjamin's was the more modulated vision of the two.

But we also must remember that the criticism Adorno levels against popular culture was shouted from the shores of a receding world. An era was in shambles. The sharpness of his many invectives (and the poignancy of his praise of Schoenberg) intimate that their spokesman saw something we do not see. Mechanical reproduction prevents us from seeing it. The unanswered question that no amount of analysis can resolve is whether the world we presently inhabit, the world from which that "something" is forever absent, can only be defined in terms of that absence. Are we as forsaken as Adorno said we were? In the final analysis, acceptance or rejection of Adorno's cultural values devolves to this question.

The next chapter on Umberto Eco gives a rudimentary technical explanation of semiology, its approach to ideology, and its reading of the aesthetic theories we have been looking at. The chapter following on Roland Barthes concentrates more narrowly on ideology and mass culture today.

Language is the Medium of Social Life

Umberto Eco speaks of "social life as a sign system."[1] This system consists of a mechanism of cross-referencing between symbols (signs, things which name and stand for other things) and existents (the objects which are singled out and designated by particular signs). The first part of the system is called by Eco the "expression plane"; the second, the "content plane." The correlation of elements from either side constitutes a "sign function." The latter is determined by the code of a language.

A code is "the individual performance of an underlying competence."[2] It is the not altogether conscious practice of language users (and the means by which they make themselves understood to one another) of substituting signifying items with their sanctified replacements, their meaning or signified. The empirical success of communication is what allows

---

[1] Umberto Eco, "Social Life as a Sign-System," in Structuralism, ed. D. Robey (Oxford: Clarendon Press, 1972), pp. 59-71.

[2] Umberto Eco, A Theory of Semiotics (Bloomington: Indiana University Press, 1976), p. 125.

writings and of this work that culture alters consciousness by way of structure rather than content, and that mass culture is a meeting ground for art and ideology.

Ever since structuralism's introduction to the social sciences in the early 1960's, some of its most prominent exponents--Roland Barthes, for example--have shown great affinities for the aesthetic theories of Bertolt Brecht and Walter Benjamin. The difference between the two generations, however, is that while Benjamin and Brecht used metaphor to express what they wanted to say (aura, estrangement), semiology uses a special terminology (signifier/signified). The creation of this terminology helps explain what structures are and how they work.

The next two chapters offer a systematic explanation of the insights excavated iu the past mages, a meta-language to think them through in. (Of course, as they are writing a language about language, they are that much more abstract, removed from naive experience.) In addition, they bring up to date the Frankfurt School's aesthetic theories of mass culture and its relationship to ideology. Whereas the early writers were intent upon demonstrating the effect of mass culture on political consciousness, and to do this they analyzed the former like a language; the later ones are more interested in proving that the relationship between mass culture and political consciousness can only be one of language, likewise our method of apprehending it.

the Frankfurt School. To structuralism or semiology (used interchangeably here), forms are the "operators" of human experience. They catalogue it, impose meaning on it, and store it for future reference. There is also no understanding of experience without them.

Hence the overall importance of semiology to other fields of social science research. No language is innocent or transparent to the reality it describes. Semiology calls intellectuals to account for the distortion their language inflicts on the reality they are examining. Its philosophy is that you cannot cure the disease with the disease, nor measure something when your tools of measurement get in the way. Its interest is not in producing new objects of knowledge, but in showing the academic world how it constitutes the ones it already has. (Benjamin and Brecht said the same thing in their own way: Do not try to coin new ideas. Rather speak about the way the apparatus does and does not let you raise your voice.)

This is largely structuralism's function in this thesis. Much as the Frankfurt School people thought in terms of form, they did not have a common language to describe the process and movement of their thought. Adorno used an Hegelian vocabulary; Brecht, a Marxist one; and Benjamin, his own very unique synthesis of Marxism and Jewish mysticism. Semiology, with its formalization of the study of forms, can be used to test and develop the idea of their

Chapter IV

UMBERTO ECO AND "SOCIAL LIFE AS A SIGN-SYSTEM"

The rallying point between Adorno, Brecht and Benjamin was the question of whether culture verified the experience of the individual--or eclipsed it. That is why, to Lukacs' amazement that anyone could _like_ dissonance, Adorno was able to respond that in dissonance, there is naming. In naming, there is release, aggression, pleasure.

Structuralism changes this question around somewhat to read, "Is it natural or is it man-made?" In the age of mechanical reproduction, ideology, on condition that it can get it to say what it wants it to say, has an ally in the image. The sight of a man and a woman water-skiing on television throbs with reality. The emotions--health, euphoria--are so close, ours cannot help but vibrate in sympathy with them. One of the ways to make sure that they do not is through a study of structure. Structure vaccinates against emotion. As Brecht understood so well, the person who stops and asks himself, "Wait--how was this made?" is interrupting his visceral response to it.

The writings discussed ahead _hone_ the formalism of

us to infer the existence of a "community" of language users (code sharers). This community is based on universally internalized linguistic laws or constants, which the individual draws messages from, according to a "rule-governed creativity."[3] It should be specified, too, that a sign does not have to be verbal. What makes semiotics (the study of signs) valuable to aesthetic theory is that it subsumes under language any structured interrelation between an expression and a content (a signifier and signified). Music, painting, gesture are all languages (sign systems) according to this theory.

The content plane of a language is the semantic configuration of the world as organized and given through the expression plane. A well-known example of the influence of language on the perception of the environment comes from anthropology. The Eskimo delineates with almost infinitesimal precision the icy substance English speakers refer to as 'snow'. In both systems, the names belonging to the respective expression planes segment an identical content ("snow") in totally different ways. The Eskimo vocabulary has words to cover degrees of hardness and color and changes in texture that the English speaker amasses into a few general phrases. Obversely, the Eskimo's perception of snow is more discriminating than the English speaker's, because his language outlines it with greater gradation.[4]

---

[3] Ibid., p. 120.

[4] Eco, "Social Life as a Sign-System," pp. 59-63.

Although the content being referred to is never tangibly present in language as such, it can be isolated or "witnessed" by cross-checking or "homologizing" the disparate expression systems. That is to say, the New Yorker understands that the Eskimo has taken the portion of the universe he identifies with snow and schematized it in a different way. In order to decode the Eskimo schema, he learns the Eskimo's system for distinguishing qualities of consistency, color, etc. When the internal relations of the Eskimo lexicon become clear, he brings its terms into alignment with his own, assuming that he has performed a similar breakdown on his own vocabulary, e.g., snow vs. sleet, soft vs. hard, etc.

Raw content never comes directly into play in language. It is approximated through a process of <u>unlimited semiosus</u>. Signs translate and are translated by other signs. Every feature of the real world that is registered in social relations does so as a sign embedded in specific, systemic relations of identity and difference with other signs. The code of a language fixes the correlations between sign "vehicles" and their train of substitutions, their "interpretants." The theory of codes is founded on the notion that language is a continuous relay, an unlimited preciosity, by which the world is made accessible through appellations and their coordinated concepts. The code dictates the polymeric links between the sign vehicle and its anchoring, reciprocal terms. It establishes the parity between the two planes. Since language is based on a "complex algebra" of substitutions, and since the interchangeability is what makes for social coherence, language is a preeminently social institution. Language is not separate from reality, but it orients us according to an independent logic of semiotic, that is to say, sign linkages. This logic is compulsive upon communicating individuals. Signification is a form of connection-making, which implies social consent. Language is the gateway to the world.[5]

The stock of semantic features (variously called markers or interpretants) that comprise a sign vehicle's meaning is called a "sememe." A sign vehicle carries a large number of signifying characteristics, as we saw in the case of snow. Some directly stipulate the external milieu, in which case they are called denotations. Others simply modify in a secondary way a previously posited sign function. They are connotations. Thus, if the Eskimo denotes the spring snow with a special term indicating "softness," a part of the environment is being directly labeled. If the subsidiary meaning of "x=soft snow" is "seasonal change," however, then the first term, the denotation, is provoking another one, a connotation, by way of association to itself rather than the world.[6]

Importantly, the full spectrum of semiotic content

---

[5] Eco, <u>A Theory of Semiotics</u>, Chapter 2.

[6] Ibid., pp. 50-55.

belonging to a sign vehicle never materializes in a single speech act. Some of its filiations come into play, others remain virtual. Still others are redeemed by some members of the speech community and not others under varying circumstances, contexts and syntactical conditions. These qualifying conditions determine which circuits will be activated, in other words, which interpretants will attach to a given sign vehicle under enumerable accompanying conditions. Many of the audience exercises in Brecht's plays were calculated to bring out often unlooked at semantic relationships.

The simplest message will ramify in many different directions on the plane of content, and for this reason Eco defines even the single word as a "text." To map a text is to break down, "de-construct," its variant readings or translative possibilities. It is to ascertain and entertain a multiplicity of coexistent semantic items, to conduct them as in a grand symphony of meaning rather than the solo of a favored, partial interpretation. A minimal expressive unit fans out into coherent subsets, called subcodes, which, in turn, overlap and connect transversely. Its content is "encyclopedic" (Eco's term), each semic feature or marker being the tuber of another sememic progression. The competencies and practices of the individual reader will usher him along one or more of these intertwining paths, signaling him when to switch as well. The structuralist analysis plays the role of the Universal Reader by registering the totality of possible correspondences and bracchiations of the signifying and signified elements.[7] Its prismatic breakdown of language is akin to the camera's breakdown of the image in optical "test."

The structuralist (sign) analysis, in other words, plots or "disambiguates" a text by spelling out its multiples, its "plural." A text's profile shows its universe of meaning without imputing it to a single subject or intention. The word /ideology/ will be decoded differently by a Marxist, a behavioral political scientist and a popular journalist. The Marxian subcode roots the term in a constellation of synonyms and antonyms--those, for example, which include the concepts "base" and "superstructure." The political scientist may disregard the interrelationships that structure the Marxist usage and, instead, consolidate the term around a set of behavioral indices which can be tested empirically. The popular journalist will probably employ the word much more loosely than either of the other two, perhaps using it interchangeably with "idea" or "belief." He will not necessarily respect the network of referrals which defines the Marxist usage or the stringency that defines the scientist's, although this will not stop his language from being enriched by the sedimentation of meaning brought about by these other, ongoing uses.

Only the structuralist analysis, which weighs these

---

[7]Ibid., pp. 140-41.

different meaning-scenarios equally, can explain what happens when a text wobbles between the more and less strictured usages. By creating an intentional ambiguity between conventionally separate subcodes, the text brings forth and exploits several conflicting resonances at once. The popularizaton and "humanization" of the technical Marxist term "alienation" is an example of such semantic cross-fertilization. A coded misuse of a code may galvanize different parts of a conceptual field at one and the same time. Sometimes this causes dissonance, other times, harmonic depth and intensity. The condensation of diverse semantic elements in one expression gives the latter its charged quality. Factoring out these elements, like factoring out the notes of the chord, intensifies one's relationship to language, which, for the radicals concerned, seems to be the main goal.

A competence that is restricted to a particular group of individuals, sometimes, as in the case of transient codes, for limited periods of time, is referred to as an idiolect.[8] Idiolects are privately held linguistic practices or bodies of practices, often patterned by class, age, occupation, geography and race. A telling example of an idiolect today is computer literacy, which younger age groups acquire as a matter of course through primary educational training. This patois makes itself felt at the mass culture level as well as in the younger generational toys which employ the

---

[8]Roland Barthes, Elements of Semiology (New York: Hill and Wang, 1968), pp. 21-3.

sight and sound designs of the new systems--music synthesizers, computer games, and the like. The significant point about idiolects, however, is that because competencies are dispersed asymmetrically throughout the population, also that any one individual may possess a multiplicity of both subcodes and idiolects (Barthes calls these skills' distributions "lexicons"), a given message <u>in its reception</u> will meet with several concurrent determinations.[9] Artists like Brecht take advantage of this fact by using audiences' native dialects to translate/alienate ideological catchwords.

From the point of view of a theory of codes, the difference between aesthetic and ideological messages depends upon each's ability to tolerate contradictory, if parallel, translations of a single text. Ideological discourse is more constrained. This is not to say that it is ever bi-univocal (no language is), or that there is not a great deal of equivocality in the way ideological statements are constructed. The point is that in ideological discourse this ambiguity is planned ahead of time in such a way as to gainsay unwelcome decipherings, to turn them into inarticulate tremors. Only those interpretations that can be predicted as consonant with the intentions of the speaker are programmed into his rhetoric. The polyvocalism of much ideological utterance in this way goes unconjugated. With aesthetics,

---

[9] Eco calls these "isotopies" in <u>A Theory of Semiotics</u>, p. 142.

as will be seen below, conflicting meanings are reflected at the level of expression.

A person's cultural background determines which subcodes he will regularly apply to the decoding of a message. "False consciousness" is a consistently partial reliance on certain safe signs. Conversely, ideology is a theoretical justification for material living conditions and social relationships that suceeds by inducing selective perception in people by narrowing their semantic range. Relying on accepted definitions, ideological argument presents an appearance of necessity through its tight sequentiality and linearity. That sequentiality, however, is obtained by closing off alternative semantic routes. The "contradictory sememic properties . . . [which can be] predicated of a sign vehicle" are eclipsed by conventional definitions, which are hammered into discourse as "names" or exclusive attributions of the expression in question.[10] In-depth examples of this process will be forthcoming in the following chapter. For now, the reader should consider what happens when an opponent of capitalism uses the verb "to liberate" as a synonym for "to steal." The speaker is making the rhetorical point that the value of the word "steal" changes with the context and semantic interdependencies in which it is enmeshed. He is announcing by his switch the nominalist character of what were taken for self-evident truths. For if as Proudhon said,

---

[10] Eco, A Theory of Semiotics, p. 293.

"Property is theft," then, indeed, to take property is to liberate it.

Now the social scientist might analyze these words in terms of the belief systems of the audience for whom they were meant. The semiologist, by contrast, draws out all of the expression's equivalences, along with the disjunctions that hold them in place. His purpose is to show in a systematic manner the existence of a selection, a weeding out, from within an assemblage of possibilities. (I.e., The word means "this . . . and not that . . .") Since any choice from within the sememic spectrum brings with it other entailments (theft has a negative status, liberation a positive one), isolating those nodal choices (how shall the original behavior be named?) pinpoints a bias that is locatable linguistically. This bias depends on the semantic roads not taken. Semiology thus defines ideology as the suppression of ambiguity. Umberto Eco says that ideological discourse is that which "suppresses the contradictory format of semantic space."[11]

Imagine ideological language to be comparable to a theatrical stage set. It is a semblance of something. One can approach its make-believe as what it purports to be. To believe the "story" is ideology. Or, one can analyze the stagelighting, the carpentry, the use of space, and through a piecing back together of all these separate structures, reproduce what was there to begin with--this time with the

---

[11]Ibid., pp. 139-42.

knowledge that it is artifice, fiction. This is structuralism. Through deconstruction, the semblance is shown to be arrived at by a long series of deliberations. It becomes a by-product. The illusion happens because of what is thrown out. The ideological statement is one that does not make manifest the criteria that have entered into the selection behind its sense, or even the fact that a selection has been made.

The aesthetic statement, on the other hand, illustrates this winnowing at the level of its expression forms. In Eco's terms, modern art chastens the general mind against ideology by incorporating the act of manufacturing meaning out of a field of choices into the final choice or representation. By making the scaffolding of the representation the subject of the representation, modern art reveals ideology's clay feet. Rather than offering a finished picture (sentence, symphony), it resolves the picture or text into its building blocks. The reader (receiver) is forced to comprehend multiple, contradictory, formalizations or orders of both expression and content. (While listening to a dissonant chord, I can focus on one of three notes without finally having or being able to eliminate the others.) He entertains not fact or fiction, but both simultaneously.

The attack on people's world visions that has come from the high art of the twentieth century has been launched by the latter's propagation of new codes, codes which irksomely cause the receiver to reflect upon the restricted nature of the old, degraded (degradable) ones. Making the laws of composition eminent betrays the seemingly simple identity of the concepts that constitute society's basic truths and assumptions about reality. The assault on the integrity of these ideas is not a philosophical or theoretical one in the sense in which Marxism as a system of thought challenges the explanatory groundwork of liberal democracy. It aims more at exposing the techniques of signification behind all forms of communication and thereby changing that communication, proving, in the breach, where and when and how the codes that we normally and unconsciously draw our messages from repress and bind. It takes us out of our habitual semiotic compulsions by disclosing concealed options.

The question a social scientist might ask in response to these reflexive investigations of art and language is "So what?" Is not reality left untouched, power relations unimpaired, when language is made its own object of inquiry? Publics may be less naive, but does this disabuse of illusion matter to anyone but a small elite, a self-annointed 'avant-garde'? Is not contemplating one's linguistic navel a quiescent activity in comparison to praxis-oriented intellectual/artistic work, which agitates against and aims directly at ameliorating specific external problems?

Eco's answer to this question lies in the way critical art involves audiences as participants in interrogating their basic routines of perception. There is a "very peculiar labor" involved in the manipulation of the expression plane of aesthetic language. This manipulation leads to new propositions concerning content. A new sign function is born out of this "labor" that is highly "original and idiosyncratic."[12] The creation of an anomalous message, in other words, reacts on the code of the language by proposing an as yet unthought of, outlawed, correlation. Although temporary, our emancipation from utilitarian discourse can inspire in us a new conceptual vision of the world by altering or suspending our basic linguistic orientations. It pushes us past our normal constraints. In sum, the aesthetic text is mindchanging because by dividing the expression plane in novel ways, it lets us known that the world can be correspondingly reorganized, that concepts are not fixed, nor the expressions embodying them immutable.

The first of the two requisite features that Eco defines as being intrinsic to aesthetic discourse is <u>ambiguity</u>. Ambiguity is defined by Eco as a violation of the language code or a self-contradiction of its rule system. Schoenberg's disobedience to the norms of harmony; Stravinsky's mechanical amplification of classical music's 'natural' sound; the Surrealists' stream-of-consciousness juxtaposition of images that appeared to have no logical interrelation, were all ambiguities in the sense defined by Eco. Deviations like these from normal discourse lead audiences to an awareness of

---

[12]Ibid., p. 261.

an "unsuspected flexibility" in language. That is, they testify to the fact that new systems may be invented to replace the old ones.

Codes are like rules of a game. Their norms are not sovereign outside their own limits. They can be displaced or added to by contrasting codes. It is easy to see, then, how easily ambiguity begets multiplicity. The purpose behind multiplicity in radical art is to place, side by side, mutually exclusive codes for invoking the same reality so that audiences can switch off between them, as if playing by several sets of rules simultaneously. To artistically destroy the founding assumptions of a genre, which radical art does, is to exemplify the fact that value and truth systems rely on completely arbitrary schemes, that meaning is versatile.[13] The purpose of the art we have been looking at has never been to convince people of a particular belief. It has been to convince people they have a choice in their beliefs.

Codes are social constructs. They are the architecture of a shared reality. A violation of a universal code is not a way of promoting chaos for its own sake, although often temporary chaos does ensue (e.g., the riots at the opening of Stravinsky's "Rites of Spring"). It is a way of making manifest to the codeusers the rules they

---

[13]Ibid., pp. 262-64. Also Umberto Eco, "On the Possibility of Generating Aesthetic Messages in an Edenic Language," in The Open Text (Bloomington: Indiana University Press, 1981), pp. 90-100.

automatically and necessarily work off of. Normal codes may continue to hold sway in the world of practical meanings even in the face of great aesthetic experimentation. Nonetheless, temporary release from them in the form of an artistic violation allows people to hear themselves hear, perceive themselves perceive, etc.

In addition to demonstrating the capacity of language for self-contradiction, aesthetic messages are self-focusing. This is the second attribute Eco assigns aesthetic discourse. A self-focusing message brings audience awareness to the contours of the language. Before Schoenberg, when listening to harmony, one saw past the scales and carpentry of the composition to the ideas they depicted. Since auratic art was thought to embody spiritual forces, one could identify these ideas with the universe itself. After Schoenberg, atonality forced a person to notice the mechanics of what he was listening to. In retrospect, harmony could no longer be heard as if it were the music of the spheres.[14]

Brecht's alienation effect also made representation self-focusing by increasing the difficulty and duration of perception. The strain of trying to recognize an object adds to our appreciation of it when we do finally figure out what it is. The gesture or the word that we have to think twice about ceases to act as the invisible conductor of an idea and attracts attention _qua_ representation.

---

[14]Eco, _A Theory of Semiotics_, p. 264.

Semiotics thus explains the maxim that in art, form and content are indissociable. The structural arrangement of the artwork is what the art is about. The expression exhibits itself as its own content. Brecht's arrested moments and pregnant gestures are ends in themselves. Like the sovereign notes of the twelve-tone scale, the fragments of the play stand on their own rather than advance the plot or embroider the scene. For language to be self-focusing, the unity of the tableau or the composition must be sacrificed. Audiences must look and wonder hard at the detritus of meaning, not meaning itself.

The same principle is at work when a generally acclaimed grammatical code is flagrantly violated. "Well they said you was high-classed, but that was just a lie," was one of the earliest (1957) introductions of an underclass subversion of formal English into mass culture. Elvis Presley's "Hound Dog" was not simply retrograde English; it was a subcoded deviation with its own contextual and aesthetic justification. It not only opposed the sterility of correctness to the "lie" of a regional, ostracized but widely used variation; it made this opposition commensurable with the utterance itself. ". . . you was high-classed . . . " is a lie, an impossibility, on the face of it.[15]

Ambiguous messages are revelatory, not because they instigate disorder, but, as Adorno stressed of Schoenberg,

---

[15] "Houng Dog," by Elvis Presley, RCA Victor, 1957.

because they flout known and utilized rules in appreciable ways. The structures of a language only become explicit after they have been transgressed. Brecht's estrangement effect recalls through an <u>unpredictable</u> infraction (of rhythm, intonation, propriety, delivery, etc.) the 'correct' way of proceeding. When a meaning misfires, the spectator is moved to account for the discrepancy. His surprise arouses his curiosity. What was he expecting in place of what he got? A reflex sends him back to the underlying rule that has been broken. In retrospect, he grasps its principle. "Aha!" one may say upon hearing five nouns strung together in a sentence, "so sentences signify because they have a subject and a predicate!" It should be clear now why Adorno insisted that radical art take off from an initial orderliness. Once art becomes completely chaotic (Stravinsky), the point is lost. Any disruption of our normal grammar should be for the sake of making the formulas of our thinking boomerang on consciousness.

Art not only renews well-worn categories. It enlarges and customizes our vocabularies by creating new ones. According to Eco, a work of art may assist people in discriminating parts of their environment that would remain in a haze if it were not for art singling them out and casting signs for them. An artistic sign function changes the code of a language in such a way as to increase society's fund of information about the world.

How does it to this? Eco explains. In aesthetic contexts, language is not used for instrumental purposes. Because of this, it can make what are generally ornamental features of a language into essential components of its message. Eco speaks of the difference on the plane of expression between form (in literate language, this would be the vocables, the phonemes) and content--the sonorous material substance that composes the sound atoms of language, namely, intonation, stress, pronunciation, etc. He states that it is characteristic of aesthetic language to become progressively delineated with respect to form:

> . . . there is a strong relation between further segmentation of the token matter of a given sign vehicle and the <u>further</u> segmentation of the expression plane of an entire semiotic system. In other words, the aesthetic experience, by revealing that within its basic matter, there is a further space in which sub-forms and subsystems can be isolated, suggests that the codes on which the aesthetic signs rely can likewise be systematically submitted to further segmentation. The pertinization of the token matter of those aspects of the expression continuum that have up to now been considered 'hyposemiotic stuff' . . . means that a work of art performs an act of semiotic redemption on its basic matter.[16]

For instance, a red flag at a political rally denotes the partisanship of the gathering, notwithstanding the shade of red. In a painting, the reddish hue used in the depiction of a flag signifies by affecting the overall balance of the composition. The difference between the two occurrences of the color red is that in the first example, red is an "optional variant" of a political signifier, while in the second,

---

[16]Eco, <u>A Theory of Semiotics</u>, p. 268.

it is a "pertinent feature" of an artistic one.[17]

The significance of this idea for popular culture is the following. In popular aesthetics, the physical dimension of language ceases to uphold the concepts that speak through it, but has new forms inscribed within its homogeneous mass. Systems (color) congeal within systems (letters). The artist refuses to stop at the word or the figure, declines to regard the ink of the typewriter ribbon through which the keys impress their mark as mere building material. Instead he explores more primarily modalities of significance, just as Brecht's actor does when he makes what, in other situations, might be peripheral factors, such as the tone of a person's voice, central to his portrayal of a social situation. In aesthetic experience, the parameters of meaning change to include more of what ideological discourse dismisses. By suddenly giving 'minor' details signifying status, Brechtian art shows what ideological appearances must repress in order to exert authority.[18]

Walter Benjamin understood semiotic 'redemption' when he remarked, "What, in the end, makes advertisements so superior to criticism" the critic asks. "Not what the moving red sign says--but the fiery pool reflecting in the asphalt," he answers.[19] Graphics disfigure the word, just as aural

---

[17] Ibid., p. 266.

[18] See Chapter 2 above.

[19] Benjamin, "One-Way Street," p. 86.

reproduction saves and inculcates fine acoustical distinctions. The word inflects in colors, shapes and sounds in popular culture. Meaning resides on the surface of language and in its vibrations. The brute dimensions of language do not simply and mutely serve cognition. They etch out their own territory of non-verbal meaning.

Benjamin's remark is a leading one. If, as he maintained, mass media subjects all forms of public address to aesthetic logic, making even politics bend to the influence of camera art, then semiotic theory demands that we stop discounting the tone of a person's voice, or the means with which he delivers his message, as frills or gratuitous additions to a more basic discourse. This being the case, we can no longer look through words to find their essence, or dismiss the accents of the "ordinary" people who support their political candidates on television advertisements, as so much incidental detail. The arrangement and lettering of a campaign slogan, or the types of people who are preselected to represent a candidate's supporters, promise to be as nuanced and fine-tuned as the substance of the campaign.

Adorno's objection to "the mere passive enjoyment of sensual sound" as an inferior form of cultural experience is both limited and vindicated by this line of thought. It is vindicated because surface effects have indeed become a part of the science of advertising. It is limited at least according to semiotics, because even the most visceral of experiences, once framed by art, enters into language and thereby becomes a conscious object of cognition. The ultimate significance of mechanical reproduction then proves to be that it has changed the meaning of meaning. It does not influence the recipient from a twilight state of semi-consciousness, as Adorno said it did, but through the ultimately ratiocinative avenue of language. Benjamin may have been sense-loving, but the objects of his sensuality were gloved in technology and, thus, rationality.

Adorno warned that art had succumbed to commodity fetishism. Benjamin reversed his warning and said that commodities are made in the image of art. Either way, the consequences are the same. If art has become implicated in many kinds of public communication, including the political, then the subversive methods we have been reading about can also become more widespread. They need not be contained in museums and galleries or remain endemic to the avant-garde. If there is no sphere of life safe from the encroachment of commercialism and commercialism combines both ideological and aesthetic elements, then there is no area safe from parody.

Indeed, Eco suggests that ideological messages can be undermined through their aesthetic component. Social and political ideas are vulnerable by virtue of their aesthetic shell. The techniques involving fragmentation, multiplicity and overdetermination can be "mainstreamed." Moreover, for people interested in political change to relegate these kinds of considerations to the backseat of "public relations," a field less important than politics proper, means they are not fulfilling their role of author-as-producer.

The possibility of effecting political change through language concerns Eco. We have already seen that he stresses the relevance of particular circumstances to the decoding of a message. He turns this insight around by suggesting that anticipating the circumstance in which a communication is to be received is a way of acting on that communication. Brecht designing his radio play in anticipation of it being jammed is an example of what Eco is talking about. Alternatively, it is possible to act on the circumstances in such a way as to steer the receiver toward variant but hidden meanings in language he hears all the time. The form stays the same, but more of its subcodes become available for deciphering and criticizing it:

> In an era in which mass communication often appears as the manifestation of a domination which makes sure of social control by planning the sending of messages, it remains possible (as in an ideal semiotic 'guerilla warfare') to change the circumstances in the light of which the addressees will choose their own way of interpretation. In opposition to a strategy of coding, which strives to render messages redundant in order to secure interpretation according to pre-established plans, one can trace a <u>tactic</u> of decoding where the message as expression form does not change but the addressee rediscovers his freedom of decoding.[20]

---

[20] Eco, <u>A Theory of Semiotics</u>, p. 86.

For example, art which makes repetition part of its point lessens our receptivity to art (advertising) which merely repeats.

This notion of a "semiological guerilla warfare" plays no part in Adorno's thinking about culture. To him what was important was that art find a way to insulate itself from market society. Art should shelter the individual from the burly-burly of capitalism. As with any discipline, the form of such an art had to be consistent and methodical on its own terms. Even the fragmentation of the atonality he so loved grew out of the imperatives of a self-referring system. That is, once the twelve notes of the scale were used up, there was nothing to keep the composer from starting over again. The music ticked off the musical moments, never achieving dramatic trajectory or decrescendo. Wherever the composition ended was arbitrary. To Adorno, this intentional lack of closure registered a note of open-endedness and hope in a world in which desire and need were decreed from above. Were the music to try to fit into the dominant culture, even as a negative force, it would lose that ragged edge, that sense of being torn apart from something larger but inaccessible.

Benjamin and Brecht changed the meaning and locus of radical art so that its purpose was no longer to provide psychological sustenance to the individual. Their vision was close to Eco's. It assumed that radical art, by altering controlling messages in accordance with the circumstances they were bound for (i.e., slowing up the pace for working class audiences), changed people's reception of them and created an overall atmosphere of skepticism toward future messages. In order to leak into the marketplace, however, radical art had to forfeit some of its independence. Faced with the problem of insinuating itself into a highly structured situation without losing its fluidity, of gnawing at existing genres without itself becoming one, it had to adapt in order to fail to adapt. It had to work <u>in situ</u>.

Benjamin and Brecht reconceptualized the role of radical art from what it had been in the earlier part of the century. Autonomous art had been able to maintain its idealism and exclusivity because it was consumed by an upper-class minority. Popular art, on the contrary, serves manifold practical uses. If a progressive popular art can be said to have had a single purpose for these writers, it lay in getting people to see, not eternal verities, as did high art, but the machinations of the culture industry: in getting people to turn around their own programming (the author-as-producer) rather than convert to a new ideology.

Both Benjamin and Brecht were clear about the fact that the most effective way to create cognitive static was to make people aware of the commercial tailoring of their thought and perception. For them, mechanical reproduction provided significant opportunities for doing this, although it also strengthened the forces of commercialism. To what degree did they believe the counterforces using their techniques represented a threat to mass culture? The answer to that question must remain ambiguous, like the techniques themselves. Judging from what they had to say, however, they never assumed that such techniques would or could bring off an ultimate transformation or revolution in mass culture. Nearer the mark would be to say that they believed a true counter culture preserved <u>some</u> "freedom of decoding" in society, a feat Adorno thought impossible. At the very least, they believed the existence of radical tendencies kept alive the populist elements in mechanical culture already specified, elements whose espousal by Benjamin and Brecht constituted a call to arms as much as it did a recognition of what already existed.

On the other hand, from the point of view of a theory of codes, it is possible to understand why Adorno balked at film and its "replica realism." For if the absence of ideology comes from putting a plethora of interpretive choices in the hands of the addressee, as Eco says, lodging in him and not the sender the task of reconciliation, then the mechanically reproduced images of mass culture are ideological in the extreme. Not only do they camouflage the process by which they have been arrived at, at the same time denying evidence of this denial. Through their endless fabrications, they are continually stretching the codes by which the prosaic is made to appear fabulous, the pedestrian--overly enhanced or ignored. The mechanical media do not affirm ordinariness. They make people apologize for and prevaricate about it.

Remember that the camera projects images with a salience missing to the naked eye. Adorno is correct in saying that mechanical reproduction locks us into a given mode of perception, developing in us a tolerance for its hypereffects which is all the more seductive (ideological) for its convincing claim to simulate reality. Nonetheless, Benjamin and Eco offer a way out of the corner Adorno paints us into. Since technology advances all the time, the lineaments of the normal as portrayed by the camera are also in a constant state of flux. As Benjamin says, "In the last analysis, structure and detail are historically charged."[21] Although synchronically, the camera denies the artifice in the images it transmits, diachronically, transitions and discontinuities in the technology betray just how important it is to our sense of what is real. The role of a radical popular art is (would be) to exploit these transitions, for example, the one between black-and-white and color film, in order to show where our most compelling images and archetypes get their power from. (The alternative a la Adorno is to become puritanical about the grip these images have on the imagination.) Showing our most treasured images in the act of obsolescing constitutes an object lesson in ideology.

---

[21] Walter Benjamin, *The Origin of German Tragic Drama*, introd. George Steiner (London: New Left Books, 1977), p. 112.

By broadening one's knowledge of social codes (dialectically, through their overturning), art can have a rather drastic effect on the individual. It can compel him to ". . . rethink the whole language, the entire inheritance of what has been said, can be said, or could or should be said."[22] According to Eco, the way language plots our choices for us can be changed if the texts challenge semantic habits cogently and persistently enough. Aesthetic texts can modify our concrete approach to the world by revising deeply ingrained cultural patterns. Radical art ". . . arouses the suspicion that the correspondence between the present organization of content and the 'factual' state of the world is neither the best nor the ultimate. The world could be defined and organized (and therefore perceived and known) through other semantic (that is: conceptual) models."[23] Language can make us rethink the ways in which the world has in the past been made thinkable.

The adversarial role played by culture then can be explained and summarized by a theory of codes. A code is the set of rules of a language which authorizes which signs will stand for different parts of the world. A sign is simply a symbol that we allow to serve as proxy for something else. A sign-system is an equilibrium between signs of relative values based on identity and opposition. Throughout this

---

[22] Eco, A Theory of Semiotics, p. 274.

[23] Ibid., p. 274.

work, the touchstone of a radical art has been whether it upsets such equilibria, setting free the individual signs (the note, the gesture, the image) in order to reclaim their meanings.

We are now in a position to understand ambiguity, multiplicity and fragmentation via semiotics. The ambiguity that has been important to the above artists and writers is really the freezing of the moment at which a system of meaning goes into mutation. Multiplicity is the piling up of many mutually cancelling systems. For example, a fragment of 'naive' harmony is interpolated into an atonal composition. Or a reader is given the full complement of semantic interconnections belonging to a single signifier. This happens in Structuralist analysis, Benjamin's concept of test, and Brecht's polymorphous use of media. Fragmentation refers to the breakdown of traditional meaning into its partial aspects, leading to what Eco called "semiotic redemption." Alternately, it can apply to a piece of art and language that always seems to be tacked on to another context, its meaning congenitally incomplete, interrupted, <u>ambiguous</u>.

Eco's semiotic treatment of aesthetic theory contributes to an understanding of the way art subverts ideology. The culture or sign system of a society determines how the material forces of that society get thought about and discussed. Art that fools with the semantic "controls" puts pressure on public dialogue. Ideology skews language in such a way as to reinforce particular class and social interests. Art ungags it, bringing into view information of importance to those aiming to transform factual reality.

Chapter V

ROLAND BARTHES: THE UNCULTURE OF IDEOLOGY

Language can either help or hinder a person master the contradictions of his environment. In saying that art does the first, ideology, the second, and that how it does it is through structure, this thesis has purposely left open the specifics about mass culture. How does mass culture reorient perception and through perception behavior? Until now, the question has been answered by warring sides. Adorno maintained that it anesthetized audiences; Benjamin and Brecht, that it brought the masses into their own.

Roland Barthes represents something of a compromise between these positions. To Benjamin, he concedes that mechanical culture is completely objective; to Adorno, that secondary meanings nestle in this objectivity (although the deception that goes on is through language, never hypnosis). With Brecht, he is of one mind that aesthetics unlock the limits of ideology. In the final analysis, he tends to agree with Adorno, but for reasons that are consistent with Benjamin and Brecht.

Roland Barthes' writings on art and ideology, while

very diverse, do consistently counterpose two sets of categories: nature versus culture, nature versus history, mankind versus society. These oppositions extend to art. A representation that resembles its object is analogical and "on the side of" nature. One that bears no resemblance to its signified is arbitrary and on the side of artifice, history. The one imitates nature. The other transforms it. The first is ideological, because it relinquishes all human responsibility behind the product. (The product may be a work of art or an institution.) The second is anti-ideological, because it stresses man's self-determination in all things. Clearly, the mechanical reproduction has elements of both. It is a facsimile _and_ a mechanical mutation of the object; nature-like and high-tech. It therefore poses a special problem to those attempting to understand more about ideology.

Barthes has numerous ways of characterizing ideology. Ideology is Doxa, public opinion, that which is treated as obvious, unsurprising, irrefutable.[1] It is also that which is repeated often and mechanically, that which exerts a "legal," "natural" dominance.[2] Ideology resembles radio in its circumambience. It is everywhere, but nobody notices it. Ideology is dead, inorganic language that comes in

---

[1] Roland Barthes, Roland Barthes by Roland Barthes, trans. Richard Howard (New York: Hill and Wang, 1977), p. 71.

[2] Ibid., pp. 153-54.

several varieties--science, religion, politics, mass culture. Each drums its message into people's heads using its own style and rationale.

Art, on the other hand, is the "detergent" people who have come into contact with the "jellyfish" of mass culture need to be dosed with.[3] Brecht is a model for Barthes. Barthes likes the fact that his critique of ideology is not pedantic or browbeating. It undermines doxic ideas through fiction and the play of language. Pleasure is an indispensable ingredient of counter ideology. In Brecht's theatre, there is no "ripening'," no waiting for ideas and themes to grow to full size in the course of the play. Everything there is to understand and enjoy about the fragment is understood and enjoyed by the time it is over.[4]

In fact, aesthetics are everything ideology is not. Where ideology is built to be repeated like a catechism, aesthetic discourse is irreplicable.[5] Where ideology weighs the signifier down with meanings that it can then manipulate at will, aesthetics divorce the signifier from the signified so that it can practice the language game aboveboard.[6] The tension between art and ideology is thus not a tension

---

[3] Ibid., p. 162.

[4] Ibid., p. 53.

[5] Ibid., p. 104. See also Roland Barthes, The Pleasure of the Text, trans. Richard Miller (New York: Hill and Wang, 1975).

[6] Roland Barthes, Mythologies (New York: Hill and Wang, 1957).

between two different political positions or sides, but one between different uses of language. (For something as subversive as semiology can always turn into a new "doxa," fossilize, reek of ritual.)[7] It is the tension between opposing cultural presences, between institutionalized and protean discourses, between commodification and creativity. The purpose of ideological language is to anchor thought in one place. The purpose of art is to return the "body" to language, to sexualize it.

The foregoing chapter should be read with these distinctions in mind. Its purposes are several. First, it expands upon Eco's theoretical discussion of the interrelationship between aesthetic form and ideology by discussing practical examples taken from mass culture. Second, it closes the circle that began with Walter Benjamin by connecting the physical characteristics of mass culture to a certain way of thinking. The press photo analysis demonstrates how the verisimilitude of the camera has become ideology's disclaimer. Third, it advances the argument that the political role of art derives from the fact that the structures of language rather than the content forge political perceptions and attitudes. This realization is particularly important in the "ageof mechanical reproduction," when content is enshrined in a mock objectivity.

---

[7]Ibid., p. 71.

The Photographic Message

In an essay entitled "The Photographic Message," written in 1977, Barthes explores the semantic structures of the press photograph.[8] He argues the conflict between its presumed neutrality and its iconic language, its nature and its culture. Ultimately, he avows that reportage is used to authenticate cultural values.

The press photograph, Barthes begins, is a message. Its components are the same as any message's. It has a source of emission, a channel of transmission and a locus of reception. The source of the photographic message is the newspaper staff--those responsible for snapping the picture as well as laying it out on the printed sheet. The point of reception is the newspaper-buying public. The message's conduit is the newspaper itself--the graphics, the lay-out, the arrangement of the text, title and caption, as well as the name and reputation of the tabloid. (The latter may color the meaning of a photograph, depending upon its political affiliations.) According to Barthes, the emission and reception of the message require an analysis of people's motives, attitudes and behavior, which properly belongs to political science and sociology. The message itself, however, deserves to be analyzed separately, since it has a "structural autonomy."[9]

---

[8]Roland Barthes, "The Photographic Message," in *Image, Music, Text*, pp. 15-31.

[9]Ibid., p. 15.

The information contained in the press photograph is constituted of two different kinds of structures--one linguistic (title, caption, article), the other iconic--the image proper. These structures work in tandem but are not conflatable. Words do not articulate the same information or inscribe the same space as shades, lines and contrasts. Barthes stresses that each system must be broken down individually before their complementarity can be understood. He turns his attention exclusively to the image since it is the lesser understood of the two media.

The distinguishing characteristic of the photograph is that it is totally literal--totally true to life. It is the case that in the transposition from the three-dimensional object to the still image, there is a change of scale, perspective and color. Nonetheless, this change does not redefine the contours of the object. Between the image and the object, there is an exact correspondence. The two are superimposable.

In language, on the other hand, the word or sign arbitrarily designates the thing it stands for. One must be imputed to the other. The physical appearance of the sign gives no clue to its meaning. For example, the word "dog" does not image a four-legged animal. To make the connection between its set of phonemes and an "actual" dog, an intermediate step must be traversed. That step is what insures the correctness of the correlation, the basis of which is not necessity, but social agreement. The reader will recognize what I am talking about as the concept of the code spoken of in the previous chapter.[10]

Now the photograph is distinguished precisely by its lack of just such a code. In other words, in the photographic message, there is no turnstile through which one passes back and forth between two unlike things--the object and its sign. The photographic image *is* the thing photographed. There is no "rule-governed transposition" between them. In other words, the photograph is analogical, not digital, like phonemes. It cannot be divided into discrete units, each unit denoting its own content. It is a continuous message. These limitations should lead us to conclude that the photograph cannot be considered a sign-system. What is troublesome about this conclusion, however, is that if it is not a sign, then its "truth" must be evidentiary rather than axiological. Yet Barthes wants to show the opposite--that we imbibe values from it, values disguised as truth.

To some extent, all analogical representations reduplicate the living object. Drawings, paintings, cinema, theatre--all bear immediate likenesses to their subjects. Nonetheless, there is always a supplementary message attached to them, a paraphrase. This supplement or rider is called a "style." Style is the felt presence of the maker. It is that which assures us that this or that reproduction has been

---

[10]Ibid., p. 16.

executed by an individual, that it is a portrait of both the maker and the subject. Even the phenomenally realistic painting sports a style--precisely that of "photographic realism." The safe thing about style is that it is purely cultural. It can only be decoded within a particular society.[11]

Barthes calls the first "bare bones" meaning of the image, a denotation; the second cultural skin, a connotation. As Eco defined these terms, the denotation singles out a part of the external world, while the connotation comments on or qualifies the denotation. In an image, the two always occur together. Their separation here is an abstraction for purposes of analysis.

The press photograph does not have this duality, however, at least not ostensibly. Metaphorical "fingerprints" are always left on the drawing, but a photograph is perceived as naked truth. The connotation of a painting can be isolated in the universally apprehended gestures, attitudes, schemes, colors, arrangements of elements, etc., which are its stock in trade. A photograph on the other hand seems to leave no room for discretion. The denotation seems to completely determine the contents. Benjamin felt this anological "plenitude" (Barthes' term) was sobering. Barthes maintains that ideas and values (connotations) somehow sail under the banner of its objectivity.[12]

---

[11] Ibid., pp. 17-18.

[12] Ibid., p. 18.

Connotation, Barthes continues, does occur in the photograph, despite appearances to the contrary. The photographic message is <u>read</u>, and where there is a reading, there are signs and a code. In one way or another, a connotation develops on top of a "message without a code."[13] A paradoxical statement. How can a photograph be both factual and value-ridden at the same time? How can it be both natural and cultural, objective and "invested"? The convergence of these antithetical elements complicates the matter of ideology for us.

The answer to this enigma must be sought in the procedures leading up to the taking of the photograph. These production-stage procedures form the basis of a code of connotation that is an intrinsic part of the photograph's material reality. The survey of them that follows clarifies their significance.

The first procedure Barthes talks about is "trick effects." He recalls a widely circulated 1951 press photograph of the American senator Millard Tydings conversing "head to head" with the then Communist leader Earl Browder. The public outrage that followed on the heels of the publication of this photograph was reputed to have cost the Senator the election. In the end, it turned out to be a fake. The faces of the two men were inserted into the bodies of two other people.

---

[13] Ibid., p. 20.

The point Barthes wishes to make is that people did not interpret the sight of these two men in conference tautologically. They placed it in a cultural frame of reference, that of an anti-Communist American electorate. The meaning the latter ascribed to the image (making it thereby into a sign) was not reducible to the immediate information registered by the image. It brought into play historically conditioned attitudes. Yet the "trick" worked because the photographic form compels belief. It seems to do nothing more than snatch a real live incident out of the jaws of time.[14]

The second procedure Barthes discusses is that of the <u>pose</u>. The example he uses is a press photograph of President Kennedy widely distributed in the 1960 election campaign. It showed him in half-length profile, eyes raised upwards, hands folded together. The position connoted spirituality, purity and youthfulness. According to Barthes, these symbols of beatitude were readily identifiable and translatable by the readership. The posture of the President was a pat one. Audiences could be relied upon to see it and fill in the appropriate meaning. (Again, it is not the fact that these values were suggested to us by the photograph that interests Barthes. It is that people infer them by reading them, by coupling signifiers--clasped hands, raised head--with specific concepts.)

Such "stock metaphors" abound in all cultures.

---

[14] Ibid., pp. 21-22.

Although their precise form changes from idiom to idiom, their ideological functions remain the same. What makes the cliches mobilized in this photograph distinctive is precisely their invisibility. There was no way to tell the connoting metaphors--the elevated head, the clasped hands--apart from the simple event. The photograph, says Barthes, was not about "the pose," but about "Kennedy praying." Its message of spirituality was communicated as though through a peephole. It was communicated as though a matter of record.[15]

Brecht's alienation-effect, it now may be seen, exaggerated the element of connotation in representation in order to give it independent density. Brecht once spoke in one of his writings about a play he had seen in the Yiddish Theatre. One of the characters in the play broke her leg. She tried unsuccessfully to collect workman's compensation from her place of employment, but the company was so tardy in responding, the leg finally healed before she got any money. The woman protested this turn of events to a sidewalk lawyer she petitioned for help.

In recounting the episode, Brecht was horrified that the actress communicated her complaint naturalistically. The line, he cautioned, should be overstated. To regret an improvement in one's state of health is surely a peculiarity. In the performance Brecht saw, the actress did not deliver the line with any more emotion than the one the character

---

[15]Ibid., pp. 22-23.

in the play was supposed to be feeling. She did not separate herself from the character in order to comment on, or express wide-eyed surprise at, her contradictory dilemma.

Taking this example, we can see that what connotation is for Barthes, attitude was for Brecht. In every ordinary communication, there is an attitude that must be ferreted out. This attitude stains the communication with history. Without it, acceptance is as automatic as it is onerous.

Objects can be 'posed' too, either by setting up the scene to be photographed in such a way as to make it look spontaneous, or by selecting the photograph to be used on the basis of its surrounding context. (The context catalyzes particular meanings from it.) Objects evoke associations (intellectual equals bookcase). They are, therefore, "stable discontinuous signs with obvious signifieds."[16] That is, they satisfy the requirements of being a language. They avoid all appearance of ambiguity. If they did not, the reader would sense their artifice. As Brecht taught us, aberrancy gives us pause. We only scan what we think we already know.

Several objects together can compose their own subtext. A press photograph of a troop of U.N. soldiers celebrating Christmas in the Sinai desert after the 1973 Mideast war traded on a number of obvious symbols: a flag

---

[16]Ibid., p. 23.

signifying neutrality; a Christmas tree representing peace; soldiers around the tree--spirituality; burnt-out tanks in the background--the paradox of spirituality and territoriality. The connotation "emerged" from these scattered signifiers seemingly accidentally, as though coming through the scene of its own accord. In fact, what "came through" was a carefully devised meaning, a signification cloaked in the appearance of a spontaneous episode.[17]

Codes presume that a message has been worked on. Hiding the semantic construction of the photograph behind its aspect of flat reporting persuades us of its truth while our defenses are lowered. It hides the synthetic portion of the message. The matter-of-factness of the mechanical "analogue," the photograph, grounds its cultural presuppositions in apodictic certainty.

Recall that Adorno complained that the "contrived objectivity" of Stravinsky's music prompted people to look for earmarks of objectivity in a piece of work rather than pay attention to the entire composition and judge its objectivity for themselves. Barthes enlarges on Adorno here by explaining how ideological messages predispose people to perceptual passivity. The ulterior meaning of an image is telegraphed through conspicuously planted symbols. These symbols are totally conventional. Yet they never appear so, because they form an organic part of a documented scheme.

---

[17] I was personally present at the taking of this UPI photograph.

(Barthes says the camera gives us the assurance of a "having-been-there.") They predigest the meaning of the scene for people. Yet people, who are certain to key into them, believe themselves to be drawing their own conclusions.

The next category of connotation Barthes analyzes is photogenia. Photogenia presents the effect of the equipment as part of the photograph's subject matter. Effects may be achieved through lighting, exposure and printing devices. Barthes reminds us that a lexicon of technical effects exists in the general spectator's vocabulary. The example he gives is of an object that has been blurred in order to convey a sense of movement and flow of time.[18]

Another example is a device used by the Lew Lehrman 1982 gubernatorial campaign. Yellowing, aging snapshots chronicling the candidate's early years were shown in the campaign's television advertisements. A photograph's physical deterioration is not a structural element of the photograph unless the photograph has been selected on that basis. Then decay is turned into a signifier, here, it so happens, of authenticity and maturity. The manifest meaning of the vintage photographs included in the television political advertisement was biographical. The latent meaning was conservativeness.[19]

Syntax is another connotative procedure. The object-

---

[18] Barthes, "The Photographic Message," pp. 23-24.

[19] Ailes Communications, 1982.

signs within and without a photograph can be read discursively, that is, as a chain of ideas. Like a comic strip, the photographic series as a whole bestows a special meaning on the individual segment or frame.[20] In Eco's terms, the circumstances in which a message occurs determines how it will be deciphered. The Lew Lehrman television advertisement is once again illustrative. There were several still shots of the candidate interspersed throughout a five-minute short. Each still unearthed another facet of the candidate's personality: family man, business executive, community leader, etc. No one of these different personae by themselves had the impact that all of them did when taken as a group.[21]

The community leader shot shared a unique syntactical relationship with the others in the series. It showed the candidate in a dark suit, standing at the podium of a large stage. The film camera zoomed in on the document he appeared to be reading from. It had an official-looking emblem on its letterhead, which the viewer was not given enough time to read. While it was in view, the voiceover announced that ten years earlier, the candidate founded "the Lew Lehrman Institute to develop commonsense solutions to governmental problems."[22]

This photograph was the only black-and-white one

---

[20]Barthes, "The Photographic Message," pp. 24-25.

[21]Ailes Communications.

[22]Ibid.

among the group. That fact, combined with the emblem and the podium, gave the photograph a press-conference-like appearance. (A photograph can signify itself as an idiom.) Alongside the other family album photographs, its colorless, journalistic, muted tone conferred on it an air of officialdom. One of Lew Lehrman's chief limitations as a candidate for governor was considered to be his lack of political experience. Through style alone, this photograph insinuated that he had been a holder of political office.

The written caption can also excite connotations in the image. Its influence hinges on its proximity to it. By being set off from the main article and placed contiguously with the photograph, the caption gives the impression of extending the visual message into words. In Chapter I, in discussing Benjamin's idea of reader "authority," Barthes was quoted as saying that a caption retires many of the potential meanings of a picture by lifting one above all the others. That point can now be seen in its wider context.

The caption functions as a connotator. Yet it is worded as if it were only a restatement of the photographic obvious. It appears to duplicate the image by virtue of its closeness to it and ease of reading. It is even treated as if it were of the same signifying material as the photograph, which of course it is not. Barthes reminds his reader that simply transferring between one medium (set of structures) and another yields new signifieds. Verbal language cannot exhaust or represent a true equivalence of the image. Yet the caption is presented as mere confirmation. Unlike the abstract painting, which leaves the better part of meaning up to the imagination, the caption denies the "Rorschach" of its description. It encysts the image in so-called hard facts.

The text is more independent and influential than its wording suggests. It can retroactively superimpose a fictional meaning on a photograph. Or it can contradict it entirely in order to offset its overt significance. Confronted with two separate messages, the reader internalizes a compromise version of the two. For example, in one segment of the Lew Lehrman commercial, the candidate appears talking to a class of students. There is a blackboard with writing behind him and a piece of chalk in his hand. He is "lecturing" about his Republican approach to education. ("Government should get back to basics just like education should get back to basics.") While he is talking, the camera zooms in on an attractive young woman in the middle row. What is happening is that the text, by flying in the face of the image shown with it, permits us to ignore the two possible explanations for the non-sequitur: The image of the woman is either a distraction and/or an illicit allusion to the word "basics." Conversely, the close-up of the woman injects libidinal excitement into the speaker's rhetoric. It may be ventured in light of this example that one reason radical techniques intensify dissonance is to shortcircuit more mild and thus more manipulative schizoid techniques like this one.

    The point Barthes makes continually is that a code of connotation is the brainchild of a particular society. Its signs are those gestures, attitudes, expressions, colors and effects that function as a universally acknowledged shorthand for larger meanings. The link between signifier and signified--the essence of any language--is forged and maintained through social usage (through what Barthes elsewhere called "the controlled exchange of the semantic relationship and collective life"). The reader has to be a member of a social contract to make the proper connections, even if they are so long-established as to seem automatic and self-evident. Like an ideographic language with both pictorial and lexical elements, the photograph communicates by way of analogy as well as speech. Only unlike the ideograph, the speech element gets lost in the facsimilitude of the image. Nonetheless, the existence of distinguishable, articulated signs that are capable of being picked out and exchanged for familiar concepts by individuals oriented to a given "cultural situation" puts the photograph firmly on the side of nurture rather than nature. Our ability to infer meanings from discontinuous symbols in the photograph gives the mechanical copy the pseudo-objectivity that Adorno complained about to Benjamin.

    Moreover, as Eco showed us, our encounter with

reality is never free from the influence of language and thus connotation. The mere fact that language divides up the world the way it does imposes categories on our thinking. Barthes refers in passing to developmental psychologists who maintain that the image is always grasped in a verbal state. Putting a name to something changes it. The world, in other words, is never encountered noumenally or "in itself." There is no pristine image, no pure state of denotation, when an object is at one with its name. As Benjamin showed, even our way of seeing is camera-like. (In another essay, Barthes defined "perceptual denotation" as the minimal comprehensibility of the image below which it would be a swarm of disconnected shapes, lines and colors.)[25] If language is the rudder of experience, and consequently connotation, inescapable, then even the technological image cannot be expected to be unfailingly impartial. The fact that it is taken to be so is one of our society's mythologies: the myth of positivity or the fact/value distinction.

In addition to "perceptive" connotation, moreover, there is the type of connotation discussed above--cognitive connotation. To repeat, cognitive connotation is made up of the lexical elements of an image, of well-demarcated signifiers that anticipate a collective readership.

Cognitive connotation and not bald description

---

[25] Barthes, "Rhetoric of the Image," in *Image, Music, Text*, pp. 42-43.

constitutes the function of the press photograph. The latter is the "alibi" of the former:

> Faced with such and such a townscape, I know that this is a North African country because on the left I can see a sign in Arabic script, in the centre a man wearing a gandoura, and so on. Here the reading closely depends on my culture, on my knowledge of the world, and it is probable that a good press photograph . . . makes ready play with the supposed knowledge of its readers, those prints being chosen which comprise the greatest possible quantity of information of this kind in such a way as to render the reading fully satisfying. If one photographs Agadir in ruins, it is better to have a few signs of 'Arabness' at one's disposal, even though 'Arabness' has nothing to do with the disaster itself.[26]

Here are the "signposts" that Benjamin talked about in Chapter I.

Conversely, appealing to the reader's culture, complex realities are condensed into legible symbols. Benjamin was distressed that the mechanical image innured audiences in capitalist society to the world's panorama rather than opened them up to it. One reason for their detachment lies in the connotation that pre-treats the images they see. Taking the above example, the totality of Arabic historical and social relations are economized in a few stock signs of 'Arabness'. These signs are do terse, the more diffuse reality that renders them typical in the first place gets pushed into the background and forgotten. The symbols displace what they were meant to amplify. Perhaps that is why somewhere else Barthes says of the political (taken in its wider, Marxian sense of

---

[26] Ibid., p. 29.

"species-being") that it is "what resists all copying."[27]

In addition to perceptive and cognitive connotations, there is ideological connotation. The former delivers information through signs. The latter ". . . introduces reasons or values into the reading of the image."[28] The ideological 'take' on the image is usually entrusted to the text, which gives the image its own, quite often, political slant. (The same photograph may surrender to completely different interpretations when placed in a leftist and rightist publication.) Nonetheless, there is no doubt that values inform the iconic image as well.

Returning to our previous example, every pose Lew Lehrman took was highly charged. Photographed arm-in-arm with his wife, the signal to the viewer was: This is a family man, loyal, virtuous and heterosexual. Photographed in a ballplayer's uniform, the message read: competition, sportsmanship, winner. In the out-of-doors, his image impressed us with his vim and vigor. Surrounded by his five children, it gave us to understand his biological and, by metonymy, political fecundity. Although each shot had a local meaning, this local meaning or denotation was only the necessary, not the sufficient, cause of the derived message. Value was introduced through "straight" meaning. Straight meaning crooked around value.

---

[27] Barthes, <u>Roland Barthes by Roland Barthes</u>, p. 154.
[28] Ibid., p. 29.

According to Barthes, a society's ideology is vested in these modes of connotation. The values of a society are expressed through its signifiers--through the physical expression forms of its sign-systems. Semiotics is useful because it focuses on the manner in which a concept is made to signify. The content of a people's ideas or beliefs in and of themselves do not capture the essence of a society's ideology, because they can be construed in anthropological as opposed to historical terms. Even a discussion of the class nature of marriage in the Lew Lehrman commercial could not clarify what was unique and time-bound about it in this context. The forms the marriage symbolism took, on the other hand, from the color film to the coordinated background music, had many temporal nuances. A social group's methods of articulating its beliefs is always idiosyncratic, even when the signifieds (e.g., marriage) crosscut many societies and time periods. Barthes thus rationalizes the reason why Benjamin, Brecht and Adorno located ideology in the specific structures of communication rather than the content: structures are inescapably and pointedly historical.

To summarize: the function of ideology is to glaze over the cultural with a false 'second nature'. Language expresses an eminently social relation. The photographic image communicates through language sub rosa. It is therefore ideological, because it buries its semantic influences under naive description.

Barthes, like Benjamin, looks at the structures of mass representation and argues that there is to be found in them a special case. Ideology in popular culture is that "which makes of an inert object a language and which transforms the unculture of a 'mechanical' art into the most social of institutions."[29] Benjamin acknowledged the hothouse nature of the mechanical image by calling it "an orchid in the land of technology."[30] Benjamin's orchid is Barthes' "message without a code." Like Benjamin, Barthes argues that there are gains and losses when we know the world through its reproduction. Unlike Benjamin, he bemoans that we have lost sight of the fact, completely forgotten, that our version of reality is second-hand, arranged, mechanical.

Both art and ideology changed under the pressure of the paradox of the "message without a code." When the image became fully adequate to the object it represented, ideology disappeared. It took shelter in the objectivity in the mechanical arts--in content. Radical art transferred its battleground with ideology to the area of technique or form, because content had become unimpeachable. Benjamin said in "The Author as Producer" that it is technique that opens art to a theory and practice of revolution. Technique is how the contrivance of the "message without a code" is made analyzable. Technique gives or takes away the prestige of

---

[29] Ibid., p. 31.

[30] Benjamin, "The Work of Art," p. 233.

truth from an image--not content. Technique is content undressed.

In addition, in "The Author as Producer" Benjamin urged that the intellectual and the artist learn to understand how they come to be expropriated of the image. Semiology comes into play here, for without a method for de-constructing the image, social scientists operate with a limited-- i.e., logocentric--definition of ideology. Taking the image apart structure by structure makes manifest the "languageness" of all culture. It extends the boundaries of analysis to the image, just as ideology is extended to the image in a new way in the age of mechanical reproduction. Without this extension, ideology must be studied strictly from the point of view of verbal language or else relegated to that nebulous area called "subliminal suggestion."

Finally, there is a utopian element in the writers we have been reading so far. It comes out most strongly in their mode and style of writing. The attraction both Benjamin and Barthes display for the fragment stems from a dislike of bourgeois technique. Both men want to rid writing of the smooth transitions, the concealed repetitions, the linear development and syntax that gird discursive reasoning. They prefer to keep language in its rawest possible state. Thus Barthes speaks of how he relishes the idea of organizing the contents of his books according to the letters of the alphabet. One fragment/idea per letter. What appeared to him about this idea was that the letters of the alphabet are arranged in a completely arbitrary sequence. Their order is totally external, but at the same time universally accepted.

Writing "parataxes" (disconnected fragments) appealed to Barthes on many levels. It divested his ideas of all and any compulsion they might have.[31] It tore down the bridges that usually convince readers of the inevitability of the author's point of view, an inevitability he found very humdrum. It saw to it that language was no longer used as an instrument of domination, but as one of pleasure. Correction: many pleasures, multiplied and permutated with each successive, "interrupted," fragment. (The "wandering" rationality of his sentences would be cut off, their meaning "exempted.") The order of fragments is aesthetic, like a flower arrangement, rather than teleological, like a thesis.[22] The lack of connection between topics is itself a form of connection. The index of a book, says Barthes, is a second text. Each thought is but an interlude of the others.

Of course, one need not accept Barthes' utopianic language to appreciate it as a counter recipe to ideological discourse and thus a caricature of what he found most disagreeable and oppressive in it. It can be no accident that all the intellectuals we have read on aesthetics longed to escape the present into a radical incoherency of language.

---

[31] Barthes, <u>Roland Barthes by Roland Barthes</u>, p. 174.
[32] Ibid., p. 70.

(Or that they wrote about their plans for escape with complete self-possession and comprehensibility.) For Barthes, too, ambiguity and multiplicity are techniques that cause well-defended categories to ooze. Multiply meaning, confuse categories by splitting them up or by flooding language with more and more of them, dismantle semantic constructions, disperse opposition--these are the ways to take the offensive against ideology. ". . . What matters is not the discovery, in a reading of the world and of the self, of certain oppositions but of encroachments, overflows, leaks, skids, shifts, slips. . . ."[33]

---

[33] Ibid., p. 69.

CONCLUSION

MECHANICAL REPRODUCTION IN THE
AGE OF MECHANICAL REPRODUCTION

The aim of this book has been to define the contribution of art to political change--art in general and mass art in particular. In focusing on structure and, within structure, the characteristics of fragmentation, multiplicity and ambiguity, it has argued the following: Art and ideology offer individuals, through their competing structural systems, different cognitive "maps" of the world. (For fragmentation, multiplicity and ambiguity imply their opposites--integration, orthodoxy, forced reconciliation.) These maps are a basis for social practice. Art is a spawning ground of new ideas. Real life is their crucible.

The distinctive contribution of this work to the literature in the field is its synthesis of two very different traditions: the Marxist aesthetic writings of the 1930s and latter-day semiotics. By bringing out the formalism in the first tradition, the structural approach made it possible to forge a collection of scattered, outdated observations into a contemporary political theory of mass culture. As Benjamin was reported to have said at the very beginning, forms change, but very slowly. Content may go through a thousand permutations, but what was structurally progressive forty years ago stands a good chance of being so today.

Conversely, by wedding the structural approach to the Marxist writings, the connection between language and political practice was made clearer. Semiology is often accused of having no relationship to practical reality. Bringing it into interdependence with the historically conscious, programmatic ideas of Benjamin, Brecht and Adorno should increase its accessibility to political science.

Lastly, this study has outlined an alternative approach to the one usually taken by political scientists and sociologists (William Kornhauser, Daniel Bell) to explain the relationship between art and politics.[1] The latter relate art to politics through the former's dependent function of either maintaining or undermining political values. The approach I have taken deals more directly with the actual art object and its relation to perception and cognition. It thus comes closer to fulfilling the role of the critic as conceived by Benjamin and the others--namely, to analyze how art in its functional autonomy casts its line into the future.

Our today is Benjamin's future. The remainder of

---

[1] Kornhauser, The Politics of Mass Society; Daniel Bell, The Cultural Contradictions of Capitalism (New York: Basic Books, Inc., 1976).

the conclusion will therefore suggest some of the ways Benjamin's and Adorno's theory can be applied to specific problems, trends and directions in present-day mass culture. The important point is that even though some of our writers have debunked mass culture for being ideological, structural analysis demonstrates that the indices of a progressive art--fragmentation, ambiguity, and multiplicity--are to be found in it just the same.

Walter Benjamin's predictions about mechanical reproduction have been borne out. It has determined our episteme, our field of knowledge, in such large ways as to be nearly invisible. Who, today, would not take the cinematic jumpcut for granted? Yet, its distortion of our sense of time and space does not appear to us to transfigure reality or plunge us into a non-naturalistic world, as abstract art does. Our habituation to it argues an ignorance of how mechanized our perception has become. This ignorance is what Adorno and Brecht determined makes people vulnerable to ideology.

The techniques that are responsible for processing what we see on television are not mere giftwrapping. They regiment and facilitate the production and circulation of a sign-system. To say this is not to oppose true and disguised reality, but to treat representation as a system of trade, as the means by which a certain image forcefully registers as the proxy of another thing. For example, a small section of a crowd on a television newscast may signify a mass demonstration or a rock concert. The choice of whether to give the viewer an aerial shot of the mammoth numbers of people in attendance or whether to contain this properly visual information in the caption will affect the perception of the event being reported on. What may happen is that in the political demonstration, the existence of coded elements like posters gives the news producer something identifiable to focus on. They relieve him of having to show the full contours of the gathering. Still, making such a gathering sensational by means of a helicopter perspective would change the signification of the news item, perhaps heightening its impact.

Since mechanical reproduction impinges on every aspect of public address, political discourse cannot remain immune to the way it recapitulates reality. For example, the United States Navy advertises for recruits on commercial television. It uses the sales pitch, "It's not just a job--it's an adventure!" The iconography lists sleek, high-speed weaponry; missiles soaring through blue skies with lightning speed; explosions resounding as the missiles find their target. The voiceover talks about the excitement and opportunities for job training and wage benefits the Navy offers its recruits. There is absolutely no mention of citizenship, patriotism or the state. A Navy career is something to be hawked. Nowhere is Benjamin's discussion of the aesthetic appeal of war and the prominence of art in our daily information better exemplified than in this commercial and others like it.

It is true one could attack the capitalist values of this advertisement. On the other hand, the angles of the photography, the montaging of well-selected signifiers, the phrasing of the spectacle, the musical score accompanying it, and the compaction of all this within a sixty-second frame, together, has the force of a meaning that is sui generis. The proof of its efficacy lies in the fact that it can say what it wants to say, even at the expense of violating normative constructs, i.e., the ones that tell us that the Navy is outside the free market and thus should not be selling itself like any other marketable good.

That advertising has a lexicon of its own independent of the political scientist's is clear at the other extreme as well. Multi-national corporations "image advertise" by selling themselves as guardians of the public interest. The private poses as public. (One might add that public interest here has no other content than that of occupying the semantic space abdicated by the state.) Corporate representatives speak the language of responsible ministers of the public weal. Private citizens play the role of "private citizens," reading from scripts but acting as though they are not, enthusing over what good neighbors chemical plants make to wildlife preserves. Their self-imposed standards, we are told, are even stricter than government-imposed regulations.

All the while, the "private citizen" acts improvisational, as candid as somebody testifying for a washing machine detergent. In Barthes' terms, the advertisement connotes its message with the appearance of the absence of all connotation: contrived spontaneity. Small doubt that Adorno thought it best for art to abandon the attempt at spontaneity altogether. How could music any longer be free-flowing, he wanted to know, when advertising and mass media--with their practiced spontaneity, their rehearsed candor--make real improvisation look like a cheap, unedited version of the real thing?

What is significant here, according to Barthes and others, is not the chimera of false promises, but the way the promises are made, the genre. On the level of the expression plane--the lighting, the coloration, the placement--produce a synthesis which succeeds or fails on its own terms. Just as one judges a play on immanent criteria such as plot, staging, direction, etc., rather than truth content, the political advertisement has its own rationality that it demands to be judged by. This rationality is internally cohesive, so that a rent in the three-piece suit of the executive standing in front of his company's map of the world, religiously spouting tenets of public accountability, might be more damaging and anomalous than a news disclosure directly afterwards about an oil spill in the Pacific Ocean for which that company was responsible. The constitutional imperatives of the television appearance seem to refer less and less to an actual state of the world. The projective techniques and conventions which structure our information decide validity. This is the reason why Benjamin and Barthes said we can unveil ideology only by means of the signifier.

The French Marxist film director Jean Luc Godard acknowledged this creeping aestheticization of politics years before Ronald Reagan became President of the United States. He appeared on American television and declared his desire to cast the President in one of his films. He wanted the Chief Executive to play himself, to impersonate the Chief Executive. The public television newscaster Robert McNeill put the same point less whimsically. He spoke of the foreign demands television makes on the non-actor, particularly the political figure. He called these requisites a "literacy" and remarked how different public men and women finesse the problem more or less ably or "fluently," to stay with McNeill's trope. For instance, Lyndon Johnson wore his television personality "like an ill-fitting wig."[2] It would be one short step from there to say that Ronald Reagan has reconciled the demands of good reproducibility with those of public office. No one could accuse him, as they did Johnson, of speaking broken "televisionese."

Walter Benjamin foresaw the increasing importance of the media when he said that the object destined for reproduction

---

[2] Robert McNeill, "Politics and Television," *TV Guide*, June 1980, pp. 5-8.

begins to anticipate reproduction. Competition in the field of public communication often centers around "state of the art" standards. The most advanced technology serves as a yardstick of literal reality. Old-fashioned equipment cannot naturalize the image as well as the up-to-date kind, because we notice it through the deficiencies in the reproduction. A "mono" record has a machine sound. A multi-component stereo sound sounds clear as a bell, transparent, "natural." Yet the latter's ultimate copy of reality specifies more than either natural perception or technically less developed reproductions. Its heightening effects shape and reshape our prevalent notions of accuracy, of adequation between the object and its synthetic reproduction. Advertising is a case in point. It delivers its message under what one advertising professional once called "the discipline of a tenth of a second." If it does not exploit the most advanced techniques, it renders its image less well. The latter comes across less economically. To be technically substandard is to communicate reality ineptly. In mechanical reproduction, what does not look real does not look rational. That is why the Punk movement in music returned to a more primitive technology. By doing that, it demonstrated how conditioned our perception is to technologically determined standards of clarity and audibility. It showed how superior reproduction is itself a form of connotation in Barthes' sense of the term.

  The implication of what Benjamin was saying is that

advertising communicates powerfully, not because of the promises it makes, but because of the ones it keeps. It is able to cram an amazing amount of information into its frame. If the fantasies it conjures succeed so well in stirring the viewer, it is not quite the same as propaganda. Propaganda is clumsy, heavy-handed. State of the art advertising vouchsafes us the truth of the fantasy--not on the plane of extention, of course, but on the plane of intention, in the attributes the image carries. Mechanical reproduction projects objects with a special vividness all its own. By amplifying their structure, it really creates a novel object for our inspection. When we turn on the television set or go to the cinema, we live in the world of the microscope. In this regard, a quotation from Benjamin that appeared in Chapter I bears repeating:

> . . . behavior items shown in a movie can be analyzed much more precisely and from more points of view than those presented on paintings or on stage . . . of a screened behavior item which is neatly brought out in a certain situation, like a muscle of a body, it is difficult to say which is more fascinating, its artistic value or its value for science.

In the political realm, this enhancement of perception through mechanical means and the emphasis on exhibition value that goes with it are frequently blamed for encouraging cosmetic and superficial values over more substantive ones. Yet, it is impossible to retreat from the more advanced point of view. The bunch of grapes in the wine commercial is appetizing, not because it misleads people about the fundamental condition of grapes--a viewer could walk into the studio at the very moment they were being filmed and taste them--it would make no difference. They will never taste as piquant as they look lucid. The reason why is because popular communication develops an art of "gourmet" looking. The structural delineation of its imagery is itself an enticement.

The political candidate is effected by how the camera structures what we see. He must function in this optic register if he is not to become the buffoon, the slapstick official. As a consequence, most candidates avoid spontaneous media appearances and armor themselves with prepared texts every time they go before a camera. Journalists complain that their public exposures are overmanaged. In the last Presidential election, political public relations professionals argued that despite the fact that the debates do not expose the issues in new ways, people watch them anyway, the reason being they want to catch the President or his opponent in a gaffe, to see him stumble. The public is, in effect, snooping on the candidate.[3]

On the other hand, every time the political candidate seeks accessibility to the mass public, he cannot avoid the aesthetic competition of mass media. To the degree that the political candidate delegates the representation of himself and his stands to the signifying apparatus of advertising

---

[3]Alexander Cockburn and James Ridgeway, "The Struggle of Edward M. Kennedy," Rolling Stone, no. 319 (1980), p. 48.

(taken in its largest sense to mean the dispensation of information), he has entered a system of framing which is not his own. The text of the President's speech is one type of signification; the foregrounding and downplaying of the camera during its presentation is quite another. Indeed, the actions of the camera produce a perceptual <u>loudness</u> that can be modulated at the will of the director. This modulation is done at least as much for aesthetic reasons as for textual ones. The purely technical and the purely aesthetic are interwoven with the substantive. Together, they contribute second-order significations. Thus, Benjamin was not only saying that the author-as-producer must innovate artistically in order to make the best use of the technical apparatus; he was, also, saying that he must understand, well enough to penetrate, society's image-sphere.

    Putting together what Benjamin and Eco said produces an interesting synthesis. Benjamin said that mechanical reproduction became the vehicle for publicizing information, and that because it was oriented to outward appearances, it draped all of our communication and utilitarian discourse in artwork. Eco added to this that art creates a whole universe of meaning out of the primary vocalic, visual and auditory traits of language. It could, thus, be argued that by breaking language down into more basic components, just as the Impressionist painter decomposed the realistic figure by means of a stipple effect, popular art preserves, promotes and elaborates criteria of signification that otherwise would have no place in social discourse. By incising new morphologies in the very space of the denotator, it institutionalizes a precision in communication that is as spectralized as the Eskimo's vocabulary for snow. It isolates and defines and enlarges the symbolic scales of many different kinds of constituencies by assigning values to natural speech variations, fixing them in a system of designation, stylizing differences. (In addition, because language, iconic and verbal, is overdetermined, it can adjoin in one image conflicting political identities--class and handsome looks, religion and a certain type of lifestyle, ideology, all may converge in one model if his type has been analyzed with sufficient care.)

Popular culture broadens the gap between the omnibus language it gleans from the universe of the common and the rarefied communication of specialized languages. This hiatus is clearest when, as in the above example, the state turns to advertising to sell itself. It cannot afford to ignore the calculated provincialism of commercial language, its rainbow of dialects, any more than a specialist could communicate effectively with laymen in his own argot. In fact, the analogy is totally appropriate. What Benjamin foresaw in "The Author as Producer" was that the intellectual must achieve mastery of this melting pot of idioms, which is popular communication, so as to transcend his parochialism.

The point is that aesthetic codes react on the entity of expression, usurping its usual symbolic functions with others related to the very appearance and body of the sign vehicle. It may be helpful to consider the analogy of a traffic report. The standard report keys in on one dimension: density. The aesthetic "report" stipulates other dimensions: the colors of the cars or, like the Surrealist Marcel Duchamp, their flower-like patterns when seen from above. The aesthetic code simply changes the relation between what is constant to what varies freely, between the parameter and the independent variable.

Both the expression and content planes of sign systems are continua which codes phrase or subdivide at different intervals. As we saw above, the aesthetic code weakens the tenability of certain concepts by segmenting or fragmenting their physical forms. These forms are the capsules of ideas, and thus ideas are made pregnable through them.

Benjamin fully understood that the "mobile articulation" (Eco's term) just described could become a source of reader independence, and that this independence enabled the average person to wrest control from the cultural establishment. Take, for instance, the fact that the word and the song are both conventional units of signification. Their codes are universally accepted. Just as popular aesthetics create suprasegmental systems of signification, they also create supersegmental ones. The commercial product is not necessarily an ultimate unit of analysis, since it can be amalgamated into, subsumed by, larger entities. Clumps of sound constitute a word, several words constitute a sentence. The same is true of mechanical culture. The elements make up the work, the work can be disjoined and integrated into larger works. There are no finished works in popular culture. There are only fragments of different lengths, some of which are called 'songs'.

For example, when the teenager presses the radio dial in his automobile to avoid an advertisement, he is redistributing the "text." With advertising or any other mechanical art, the consumer half of the relationship must always be considered. Any discussion of commercials that treats him as passive and reactive fails to take into account that the consumer has counterstrategies, strategies which derange the message of the advertiser. To prove that these actions are not without impact, one need only look at the reaction of the advertising industry. It invents codes that neutralize the neutralizing moves of the consumer. In response to the button-happy teenager, it writes commercials which sound like part of the substantive programming content. It tries to slip them past the consumer's notice--to hide the discontinuity by means of simulating a code that is not its own. The teenager responds by writing music which sounds like commercials. This back and forth imitation does, indeed, constitute, to use Eco's phrase, "semiological guerilla warfare."

The end result of this warfare may be the strenghtening of the individuality Adorno believed was doomed by the mechanization of art, but which Benjamin believed was simply undergoing metamorphosis. Take the contemporary popular 'genre' called "turntable jazz." The disc jockey or "mixer" improvises with recorded music in an analogous way to the jazz musician. His instrument is not a saxophone, however, but a multi-speaker, multi-turntable panel, and his 'riffs' do not come out of a horn but are excerpts of popular songs intermingled and overdubbed with other popular songs. As the formats of popular music radio stations become increasingly standardized, as songs become more and more formulaic, consumption strategies develop to circumvent this growing uniformity. The commercial product becomes the raw material for somebody's independent coordinations.

The auratic work of art could not tolerate such tampering. It was organic and quasi-sacred. On the contrary, the mechanical work is modular to begin with. It can be added to, or subtracted from, without harming its essential nature. Thus, Benjamin argued that the beneficiary of manufactured culture is the average recipient, who is no longer confined to the receiving end of culture. Technology not only involves the bystander as participant. It encourages a 'do-it-yourself' attitude toward art in which the distinction between them all but disappears.

What is most important about this multilation of the

commercial entity, at least for our purposes, is that it is basic to the logic and apparatus of mechanical reproduction. The liberty to cut, splice, arbitrarily juxtaposition and overlay is mechanical reproduction's freeing aspect, its peculiar form of license. Mechanical reproduction has "jazzed" modernity. This is precisely what disturbs political scientists about political advertising. They complain that the dignity of the office is compromised when the public sees the President "pop up between the deodorant and the dog food."[4] That was exactly Benjamin's point. From the perspective of a critical popular culture, the most exciting possibilities of art lie in the perversities of its connections, in the image's total lack of sovereignty over its context. It is clear from the above example, too, why Benjamin said we have to count as potentially revolutionary these makeshift alterations of official culture. Incipient and incidental forms of art represent an individualized remodeling of commercially orchestrated options.

It is this freedom of construction and de-construction that led to the dissolution of the great artistic traditions Adorno deemed so important. Surrealism exploited this freedom by creating an ingeniously irrational art whose very irrationality was an assault on the bourgeoisie. Adorno

---

[4]Bernard Rosenberg and David Manning White, eds., Mass Culture: The Popular Arts in America (London: New Left Books, 1961), p. 3.

retreated from its anarchy (he did not trust that the unconscious had not also been colonized) onto the solid ground of Schoenberg's method. In the latter, every note was assigned its proper place. Nothing was thrown together pell-mell. The irrational was put into a straitjacket.

Surrealism was not alone in its reaction to the structural opportunities unlocked by mechanical reproduction. In the American South, the desacralization of folk idioms brought about by technology led to the cross-fertilization of traditionally segregated idioms. The first time audiences heard a saxophone in a Country-Western or "hillbilly" song, for example, it sounded odd, impermissible. It was as though audiences were hearing the instrument for the first time. The reason: "R & B" (rhythm and blues) was black ethnic music; hillbilly was white. The saxophone had been strictly associated with the former. When it suddenly began to be used differently, anomalously, in the studio, long-time assumptions began to crumble. The result--rock and roll--intimated the possibility of other kinds of racial integration. The one fact that should not be lost sight of, with regard to the parallelism between two movements that otherwise had nothing in common, Surrealism and rock and roll, is that they were both exploitations of structural changes in the means of representation. New ways of seeing and hearing came out of each's crossing of limits.

Of course, Adorno's misgivings about this new freedom

haunts us today. Surrealism's audacious syntax has since been taken over by advertising and commercial film simply to shock rather than express more profound social currents. Rock and roll serves as background for beer--or political candidate--commercials. This should not come as a surprise. The source of mechanical reproduction's freedom is the source of its potential for commercialization.

The commercial applicability of most technically progressive art is sobering. The rock and roll music that introduced and concluded the Lew Lehrman advertisement examined in Chapter 6 was considered by the candidate's campaign manager to be the most important part of the commercial. In response to favorable feedback about it, a one-minute spot was created and aired that was composed entirely of the fast-paced music and a montage of visuals of the candidate shaking hands with people, visiting fairgrounds, running, etc., all in time to the beat.[5] The explanation of the candidate's stands was entirely cut out so that the music could play and maintain a high level of tension throughout the segment. As Barthes says, it is the signifier that is telltale.

With the power of editing endemic to mechanical reproduction goes the power of inclusion. Mechanical reproduction is able to democratize, to redraw, the boundaries of selection

---

[5] Personal communication with campaign manager, Charles Degliomini.

Cage's revelation of the infinity of raw material at the artist's disposal, there is a social pattern of agreement about its completeness. In every so-called simple reflection of reality, even in the infallibly reproduced image, there is an institutionalized level of focus. The latter will determine the degree of exactitude with which an object or universe of objects will be depicted by the popular media. What is worthy to appear? This is a qualifying (i.e. ideological) decision, one that will be answered differently by different contributors, and which will find different kinds of acceptance in different kinds of audiences.

Brecht saw theatre as a way to restore the texture of our experience. He probed what happens to our authority to represent our own experience, to "author" it as Benjamin would say, when it is constantly and relentlessly subjected to uniform procedures and conventions that redefine its figuration and thus belie its specialness. In the presence of 'realistic' procedures that mechanically process and heavily connote experience, 'truth' may often be invested in the slender play of nuance Brecht recreated on stage in the tone of a person's voice at a particular moment or a passing gesture.

Brecht worked in an auratic art form--theatre. The fact is, however, that the atmosphere and environment in which we live, littered as it is with pieces of mechanical reproduction, offer ready-made contradictions to capitalist culture.

There is multiplicity in the air. The polyglot sounds one is bombarded with walking down a crowded city street is the experience Stravinsky captured in his music and the one much modern art imitates. Through the collision of idioms in real life, people acquire a tolerance and appetite for heterogeneity, for cacophony. Now in capitalist culture, different kinds of music are generally channeled into separate formats so as to best exploit their listening markets. Homogeneity in listening is the rule. But Stravinsky-like crossovers and fusions between musical types happen all the time on the grassroots level, despite radio programming. When they happen, their music becomes the mark of a progressive art. A strictly formal innovation--entangling commercially segregated idioms --becomes a statement of defiance against having one's tastes molded by what is most profitable.

If jazz and rock air on separate ratio stations, but play next to each other in a city park, then their containment by radio will seem, not so much pernicious, as needless, irrelevant. The experimental material that evolves in local, uncoded places like the street and transient nightclubs disestablishes market categories. Such experimental music is seldom aired on mass radio on account of its generic ambiguity. Needless to say, it is this ambiguity, this crossing of borders, of dissonance-cum-harmony, which the avant-garde cherishes, for it represents an aesthetic response to an institutionalized symbolic limit. In essence, the diversity between what simply happens and what will be remembered as having happened. Not only does it put politicians and dog food on an equal par, it proves equally indiscriminating (vigilant) of the noteworthy and the forgettable. It can turn anything--even the most unremarkable sights and sounds --into signs, into language. Whatever mechanical processes "notice and publish," no matter how incidental it may have seemed at the outset, suddenly takes on the status of representation.

Umberto Eco describes this sort of sign production as ostention:

> Ostention occurs when a given object or event produced by nature or human action (intentionally or unintentionally) and existing in a world of facts as a fact among facts, is 'picked up' by someone and shown as the expression of the class of which it is a member.[6]

The entire world becomes a prospective text before the aggressive semiosus of mechanical reproduction.

The lesson Brecht bequeaths to us is that just as methods of sabotage are developed against monotony, they can be mobilized against prevalent hierarchies of emphasis. The line between major and minor, significant and insignificant, language and noise, can be floated. It is demonstrated by Brecht to be socially determined, arbitrary, displaceable. Everybody is his own historian. The reader is the expert. The cut-off beyond which representation becomes impossible,

---

[6] Eco, A Theory of Semiotics.

surplus, is ideological, just as the commercial product as a starting point of analysis is an ideological fiction. Then, too, the idea of ostention can provide another defense of the fragment. With text everywhere, our representations of the world are nothing more than random sightings.

The combination of technology and aesthetics can be used to undermine what is commonly considered knowledge. Art uses technology to stretch the limits of palpability and propriety. Thirty years ago, the experimental musician John Cage went to the laboratories at Harvard University to monitor the sounds of his own nervous and circulatory systems. He discovered in its soundproof chamber an absence of taciturnity. There is no silence, he said, only "non-intentional sounds." More recently, the expermental artist Yoko Ono called attention to the 'politics of sound' by putting the sound of a sexual orgasm on one of her records. When criticized for immodesty, she defended her move with an Eco-type explanation. The public, she argued, is routinely exposed to the sounds of bombs exploding. Censoring the sounds of intimacy would be an unbalanced omission, a knocking out of part of the range of human behavior that is offered for public perusal. The absence of silence, the absence of exception--both of these ostentatiously made points attack normal assumptions about reality by showing what it has to repress in order to gather to itself an identity.

In every portrayal, we have only to conclude from

of radio or any mainstream medium is a planned, inorganic diversity, a similacrum of the prolific diversity representative of music's true use value. Adorno predicted that our musical sensibilities would adjust to and accept this rationalization for capitalist profit. Barthes and Benjamin thought that the exasperating complications of the avant-garde constituted a subterfuge against it.

Indeed, ordinary consumers subvert the text in much the same way the revolutionary producers do. (Again, Benjamin turns out to have been prophetic in having obliterated the distinction between these two.) Benjamin's quarrel with Adorno rested on the fact that no matter how exploitative and routinized a commercial product may be in the planning and selling, people consume it in all sorts of audaciously non-directed ways. The consumers who walk down busy thoroughfares with "big radios" atop their shoulders do represent a form of cultural resistance if we think of them as circulating and thus recomposing sound. Even when culture is consumed lackadaisically--Adorno would surely castigate disco music for becoming the unconscious pulse of our work life-- the situation can be turned around. Raising the volume (punk) or complicating the rhythm (funk) may make us think about the ways ambient mass culture lubricates our private and work lives.

Although the stands taken by Benjamin, Brecht and Adorno toward different kinds of art remain irreconcilable as such, perhaps it is not the specific art that matters. (After all, Benjamin implied that by the time art congeals into a recognizable genre, it has outlived its revolutionary usefulness.) Perhaps revolutionary art can be described generically--through structure, reduced in this way to its underlying ambiguity, multiplicity and fragmentation. For example, a popular or grass-roots response to existing foreclosures in popular representation, including segregation by race and taste, falls under the category of ambiguity. When local grafts that are proscribed by the media develop spontaneously in the activity of consumption--the productive activity--Benjamin's ideas can be seen in action. Benjamin, by the way, was the first to say that the masses' tastes were naturally surrealist, so that he probably would not be taken aback by such "guerilla" actions. Nonetheless, these characteristics can be inverted, as when a context (neo-expressionism) is supplied a fragmentary, marginal art form (graffiti).

And yet the dirge Adorno wrote for autonomous culture can still be heard in those brief moments of silence when we evict mass culture from our lives. In the stillness, we remember that he said that mechanization obscured art's origin in the human soul; that it cultivated in people a taste for harshness, violence and conformity. After reading Adorno, one notices that when one turns on a rock radio station, it is difficult to tell the difference between the songs and the advertisement. One notices that the tempo of much popular music *is* assaultive. It captures a person in its driving repetition, whether he wants to be caught or not. (It is no doubt easier to surrender than to fight its physical persuasion.) The effect is physiological. The beat controls the listener, as advertisers surely know. The more electronic it is (disco), the more irresistible is its inhumanly even and high speed rhythm. Mass culture's dragnet around the individual tightens with each step forward in technology. (Already rock and roll percussion is beginning to sound weak, desultory.) On the other hand (Benjamin again), this is the music of the streets--the music that can turn the drill of construction and the whinny of a garbage truck into "text."

This work has attempted to reopen the questions first broached by the Marxist writers of the 1930's concerning the political prospects of mass culture. If it seesaws between the views of Benjamin and Adorno on the question of mass culture's revolutionary value, it is because both men succeed so well in convincing us of its positive and negative points. The goal has not been to reach a final verdict about mass culture, so much as it has been to define its forked significance for political consciousness. It is only fitting that a work about ambiguity end in ambiguity.

SELECT BIBLIOGRAPHY

Writings by the Authors

Theodor Adorno

The Authoritarian Personality. New York: W. W. Norton & Co., 1950.

"The Fetish Character of Music and the Regression of Hearing." The Essential Frankfurt School Reader. Edited by Andrew Arato and Eike Gebhart. New York: Urizen Books, 1978, pp. 27-300.

Negative Dialectics. New York: Seabury Press, 1973.

The Philosophy of Modern Music. New York: Seabury Press, 1977.

"Perennial Fashion--Jazz." Prisms. Translated by Samuel Weber and Shierry Weber. London: Neville Spearman, Ltd., 1967, pp. 119-32.

Roland Barthes

Elements of Semiology. New York: Hill and Wang, 1968.

Image--Music--Text. Translated by Stephen Heath. New York: Hill and Wang, 1977.

Mythologies. New York: Hill and Wang, 1957.

The Pleasure of the Text. Translated by Richard Miller. New York: Hill and Wang, 1975.

Roland Barthes by Roland Barthes. Translated by Richard Howard. New York: Hill and Wang, 1977.

Walter Benjamin

Illuminations. Edited by Hannah Arendt. New York: Schocken Books, 1969.

"Brecht's Characters." *New Left Review*, no. 123, September 1980, pp. 92-96.

The Origin of German Tragic Drama. Introduction by George Steiner. London: New Left Books, 1977.

Reflections. Translated by Edmund Jephcott. New York: Harcourt Brace Jovanovich, Inc., 1978.

Ernst Bloch

With Lukacs, G.; Brecht, B.; Benjamin, W.; and Adorno, T. *Aesthetics and Politics*. Translated and Edited by Ronald Taylor. London: New Left Books, 1964.

"Benjamin's Philosophical Cabaret." *New Left Review*, no. 116, July 1979, pp. 94-96.

Bertolt Brecht

Brecht on Theatre. Translated by John Willet. New York: Hill and Wang, 1957.

Umberto Eco

The Open Text. Bloomington: Indiana University Press, 1981.

"Social Life as a Sign-System." *Structuralism*. Edited by D. Robey. Oxford: Clarendon Press, 1973, pp. 59-71.

A Theory of Semiotics. Bloomington: Indiana University Press, 1976.

Max Horkheimer

Critical Theory. Translated by Mathew J. O'Connel and others. New York: Herder and Herder, 1972.

With Adorno, Theodor. *Dialectic of Enlightenment*. New York: Seabury, 1972.

William Kornhauser

The Politics of Mass Society. New York: The Free Press, 1959.

Georg Lukacs

"On Bertolt Brecht." New Left Review, no. 111, April 1977, pp. 77-80.

Herbert Marcuse

Negations: Essays in Critical Theory. Translated by Jeremy Shapiro. Boston: Beacon Press, 1968.

Secondary Works Consulted

Buck-Morss, Susan. "Walter Benjamin II." New Left Review, no. 109, September 1982, pp. 77-95.

Bramson, Leon. The Political Context of Sociology. Princeton: Princeton University Press, 1961.

Culler, Jonathan. Ferdinand de Sassure. New York: Penguin Books, 1977.

Eagleton, Terry. "German Aesthetic Duels." New Left Review, no. 107, January 1978, pp. 21-38.

Habermas, Jurgen. "Modernity vs. Post-Modernity." New German Critique, no. 22, December 1981, pp. 3-14.

Jameson, Frederic. The Prison-House of Language: A Critical Account of Structuralism and Russian Formalism. Princeton: Princeton University Press, 1972.

Jay, Martin. The Dialectical Imagination: A History of the Frankfurt School and the Institute of Social Research, 1923-50. Boston: Little, Brown & Co., 1973.

Kramer, Hilton. "Today's Avant-Garde Artists Have Lost the Power to Shock." New York Times, 16 November 1980, sec. 2, p. C11.

Rosenberg, Bernard and White, Manning, eds. Mass Culture: The Popular Arts in America. London: New Left Books, 1961.

Wolin, Richard. "From Messianism to Materialism: The Later Aesthetics of Walter Benjamin." <u>New German Critique</u>, no. 22, December 1981, pp. 89-109.

DATE DUE

DEC 1 3 1991

DEMCO 38-297